Courtesy Florence Beaujean

# MUSIC FOR EARLY CHILDHOOD

*Moving incessantly . . . moving all day long . . . discovering himself, his capabilities, his relationship to his environment. A board becomes his gangplank to transports of delight. An empty nail keg serves for a drum; the pounding sounds he makes are sweeter far to him than the music of any symphony orchestra. This is the child who comes to us, bringing his faith, his zest, his music, and all the other characteristics of early childhood.*

# MUSIC FOR

**NEW MUSIC HORIZONS SERIES**

# EARLY CHILDHOOD

OSBOURNE McCONATHY · RUSSELL V. MORGAN
JAMES L. MURSELL · MARSHALL BARTHOLOMEW
MABEL E. BRAY · EDWARD BAILEY BIRGE
W. OTTO MIESSNER

SPECIAL EDITORS

*MARY JARMAN NELSON* AND *GLADYS TIPTON*

ILLUSTRATED BY

*Lillian Chestney* AND *Ellen Simon*

## Silver Burdett Company

NEW YORK    CHICAGO    DALLAS    SAN FRANCISCO

# ACKNOWLEDGMENTS

Books like this are not just written—they grow! They grow from the observations and experiences and creative efforts of many people. They are rooted in the accumulated knowledge and insights of the past and the exploration and experimentation of the present. Literally, legions of people have contributed to their making.

Well over a hundred years ago, Friedrich Wilhelm Froebel, in founding the kindergarten movement in Blankenburg, Germany, contributed to this book. So did people of Norway, long before that, when they created the lovely folksong, "Now Sleep Gently." Recent study of child development that has been taking place in research centers in various parts of the country has also contributed. And so have the well-known contemporary American composers Marion Bauer, William Grant Still, and Norman Lloyd. Indeed, the makers of this book are indebted to untold numbers of teachers, parents, musicians, researchers, and children—past and present—who are directly or indirectly responsible for some aspect of the present volume; and they wish to make this obligation explicit. For practical reasons, however, only those directly involved can be mentioned.

First and foremost, the contribution of the two consulting editors must be recognized. It is no exaggeration to say that without the numerous ideas, the creative work, and the unstinted effort of Mrs. Mary Jarman Nelson (Rollins College, Winter Park, Florida), many of the outstanding musical and educational features of this book would not have been possible. The original materials and thoughtful suggestions of Dr. Gladys Tipton (University of California at Los Angeles, California) have added immeasurably to the quality of the volume.

It is an exciting experience to see creative musicians working hand in hand with educators to create music which is suitable for young children and sufficiently simple for the classroom teacher to play, and yet which is in itself artistic. This occurred time and again. Miss Marion Bauer, dean of American women composers, and Mrs. Sally Tobin Dietrich, composer of children's music, applied rigorous self-control to their compositional techniques in writing accompaniments for songs in the book. And Dr. William Grant Still was no less careful in composing "Animal Sketches." An achievement along this same line was accomplished by Mr. Norman Lloyd (Juilliard School of Music, New York), in his non-technical treatment of the subject of improvisation.

Head of our "Watchdog Committee" was Mrs. Miriam Brodie Stecher, Harriet Johnson Nursery School, New York. She has given ideas unstintingly out of her rich experience, seen to it we served the child.

Among the numerous teachers and educators who suggested materials and offered valuable ideas and criticism to us are Mrs. Erma Hayden (Fisk University, Nashville, Tennessee), Miss Esther Hubbard (State Teachers College, Oneonta, New York), Mrs. Madeline S. Levine (New York University), Mrs. Fred B. McCall (Chapel Hill, N. C.), Miss Claire Coble (Day Care Center, New York), Miss Esther R. Collyer (Allen County Public Schools, Fort Wayne, Indiana), Mrs. Gladys Peters (Cleveland, Ohio), and Miss Dorothy Hickok (State Teachers College, Oswego, New York).

Much of practical value was gained through observation in kindergartens and nursery schools. Of special interest was the work of Mrs. Hermine Dudley (Ethical Culture School and the Conservatory of Music Education of New York), Mrs. Evelyn H. Hunt (Dalton School, New York), Mrs. G. Gaines (Church of All Nations Nursery School, New York), Mrs. Erma Hayden (substituting for Charity Bailey at The Little Red School House, New York), Mr. Phillip Merrill (Hoff-Barthelson Music School, Scarsdale, N. Y.), and Mrs. Hortense Jones (Harlem River Nursery School, New York).

Mrs. Nelson's associates, Miss Barbara Ziegler and Miss Sally Monsour, helped test materials.

Recognition is also due the following specialists: Mrs. Edna H. Doll (Clifford J. Scott High School, East Orange, N. J.), for consultation, and use of her "Variations on a Walk," and "The Tired Giant"; Mr. Phillip Merrill for his evaluation of phonograph records; and Mrs. L. Lorraine Penland (assistant to Dr. Arthur Jersild, Teachers College, Columbia University, New York), for thoughtful criticism of the manuscript.

Finally, credit is due Mary Whitcomb for the important part she has played in writing continuity and in general "seeing the publication through."

# CONTENTS

*Introducing Jean and Robin and other children in Miss T.'s classroom; with songs that aid their development and the whole school program.*

*Presenting Miss T.'s children at block time, rest time, and on the playground, and finding movement the keynote of a day that is winged with song.*

*Utilizing the children's own patterns of movement in order to develop a readiness for following the patterns set by music.*

*Having freely explored the sounds made by various instruments, Miss T.'s children are ready to use these sounds. With notes on children's piano-playing.*

*Containing suggestions for listening experiences that serve the child during his preschool years and the years to follow.*

*Stories with a cast of characters that includes every child that listens to them, since they offer participation.*

*Songs that add to the children's enjoyment of Halloween, Thanksgiving, Christmas, and other holidays.*

*Songs for the Years, for singing at home around the family piano; with notes on the interrelationship of school and community.*

*PIPING, STRUMMING and DRUMMING, by Mary Jarman Nelson IMPROVISATION, by Norman Lloyd A SUMMARY, by Gladys Tipton WHEN COMPANY COMES*

# CREDITS

Special acknowledgment and credit are due for permission to reprint the following materials:

"The Allee Allee O" and "Two in the Middle": From HULLABALOO AND OTHER SINGING FOLK DANCES, collected by Richard Chase, copyright 1949. Used by permission of Houghton Mifflin Company.

"Burlesque Band" (page 68), "Mister Fox," and "My Mother Sent Me": From MUSICAL GAMES FOR LITTLE ONES, collected by E. C. Griffiths. Used by permission of Evans Brothers Ltd., London.

"Dance to Your Daddy": From CHILD SONGS OF HAWAII, published 1923 by C. C. Birchard and Company. Used by permission of Bessie C. Bowdich.

"Down in the Valley" and "The Lonesome Dove": From THE SINGIN' GATHERIN' by Jean Thomas, the "Traipsin' Woman," and Joseph A. Leeder; published 1939 by Silver Burdett Company.

"Drop the Handkerchief": Used by permission of the Oliver Ditson Company, from the book, OLD TUNES WITH NEW RHYMES.

"Everybody's Welcome": Adapted from version in SONGS OF THE OLD CAMP GROUND, compiled by L. L. McDowell.

Folk dance from HANSEL AND GRETEL by Engelbert Humperdinck: By permission of G. Schirmer, Inc.

"A Happy Band" ("Jump and Hop"): Reprinted from MUSIC, BOOK TWO, by Lena Milam, copyright 1951 by The Steck Company.

"Hop Up, My Ladies": Reprinted from OUR SINGING COUNTRY, collected by John A. and Alan Lomax, published by The Macmillan Company.

"Lily, Lily Wallflowers" and "I Have a Bonnet Trimmed with Blue": From SINGING GAMES by Alice E. Gillington; "The Fox Jumped Up": From TRADITIONAL NURSERY RHYMES, edited by John Graham; "This Old Man": From ENGLISH FOLK SONGS FOR SCHOOLS, collected and edited by Cecil Sharp and S. Baring-Gould. These materials are used by permission of J. Curwen & Sons, Ltd., London.

"Little Wind": Words reprinted by permission of Frederick Warne & Co., Ltd., London; from UNDER THE WINDOW by Kate Greenaway.

"The Marines' Hymn": Used by permission of the United States Marine Corps.

"Norwegian Lullaby" ("Now Sleep Gently"): Reprinted from LULLABIES OF MANY LANDS by Dorothy B. Commins, published by Harper and Brothers. Copyright 1941 by Artists and Writers Guild, Inc. Used by permission.

"The Old Brass Wagon": Reprinted from THE PLAY-PARTY IN INDIANA, by Leah Jackson Wolford; by permission of the Indiana Historical Bureau.

"One More River": Reprinted from OZARK FOLK SONGS, collected by Vance Randolph; by permission of the State Historical Society of Missouri.

"The Orchestra": From FIFTEEN TUNES FOR FRIDAYS, by Mary Jarman Nelson, published by Creative Music Publishers. Used by the permission of William O'Toole.

"Le Petit Chat" ("The Little Cat"): Melody from CHANSONS D'ENFANTS by S. Brés and Laure Collin, by permission of Librairie Delagrave, Paris.

"Round the Christmas Tree": Music by C. Ramos, through the courtesy of Sociedad de Autores y Compositores de Mexico, Mexico City.

"The Shoemaker": From ENGLISH FOLK SONGS OF THE SOUTHERN APPALACHIANS, by Cecil Sharp and Maud Karpeles; "Canon" ("Dolly's Lullaby"): From MUSIC AND MOVEMENT by Ann Driver; "Cadet Rousselle" ("Skipping Merrily") and "Boutique Fantasque": From POLICHINELLE, compiled by J. R. Monsell. These materials are used by permission of Oxford University Press, London.

"The Sky Is Falling" ("Chicken Licken"): Words reprinted by permission of American Book Company, from MANUAL FOR FIRST GRADE MUSIC by Robert Foresman.

"Song for Hanukah": From THE SONGS WE SING, published by the Commission on Education of the United Synagogues of America. Used by permission of Harry Coopersmith.

"Today's the First of May": Melody and words reprinted from THE SONG PLAY BOOK by Crampton and Wollaston, by permission of A. S. Barnes & Company.

"Willowbee": Reprinted from PLAY SONGS OF THE DEEP SOUTH, collected by Altona Trent-Johns. By permission of Associated Publishers, Washington, D. C.

We are indebted to the Library of Congress for the following songs from its collection of field recordings: "Knock Along, Little Rabbit," "Little Red Bird," "O Daddy Be Gay," "Old Gray Horse," "One Day One Foot Went Moving," "Shanghai Chicken," and "The Singing School."

"Ki-yi-yi-yi," and "Hippopotamus," by Mary Blatt Koch, were originally printed in *Playmate Magazine* and are reprinted here.

"O ro bog liom i" ("Jump, Jump, Jump"): The melody is reprinted from NURSERY RHYMES ARRANGED FOR VOICE AND PIANO, collected by Carl Hardebeck and published by Municipal School of Music, Cork.

My friends living in a small town where I often go know that I am interested in music, and particularly in music for children. So it was natural for them to tell me about the musical activities of a certain Miss T., who is in charge of the pre-school group at the local elementary school. (I call the young lady "Miss T." chiefly for the reason that her name does *not* begin with T!). From all that was said I gathered that Miss T. was putting into practice many of the ideas we wished to embody in this book, which was then in preparation. I was very much intrigued and decided that if possible I would see with my own eyes what was going on.

One afternoon I phoned the school principal for permission to visit and explained what I had in mind. What would be the best time of day to see some of the musical activities, I inquired.

"Well, there really isn't any set time for music in our pre-school," the principal answered. "Miss T. introduces it quite informally all through the school period, and uses it for all sorts of purposes and occasions. The truth is that any time may be music time with Miss T. and her children. That makes it a bit hard for a visitor, although you'll be very welcome. But you'll just have to take potluck."

This in itself sounded very promising, in spite of the slight problem about my schedule. I hoped to find evidence to support one of the most important ideas we wanted to incorporate in the working plan of this book; for our plan was to choose material and organize it to help teachers weave music into the whole school life of their children. Far too many teachers think of music simply as a separate subject, to be taught at a stated hour and then forgotten for the rest of the day, if not for longer than that. Evidently Miss T. had quite a different approach. My prejudice in her favor was decidedly strengthened.

Next day I went round to the school prepared to stay as long as need be. Yet when I arrived I found what seemed at first sight a regular music period in full session, in spite of what the principal had said. I came a few minutes late, and as I approached Miss T.'s room I was greeted by the sound of singing. Even through the closed door it sounded very wholehearted and joyous. My entry hardly caused a ripple. Miss T. herself, who was singing along with the children, threw me a quick glance and a smile; but the children took no notice whatever. Everyone was too much taken up with making and enjoying music. Not everybody was singing, yet it seemed to me that everybody was joining in. Two girls and a boy were moving about freely, "expressing" the music with feet and hands, arms and legs, heads and bodies. One boy was using rhythm sticks and a girl was manipulating

*The search begins
for ideas tested by
successful practice*

*Miss T. is visited
although she has no
regular music period*

sand blocks. A few of the children, busy with paints, were "just listening," but I didn't get the slightest impression that they were being left out. There seemed to be no compulsion—just a situation in which everyone felt encouraged to sing just as freely as he wanted to, when and if he wanted to.

(That, of course, is exactly the kind of situation which this book is designed to promote. The material it contains, both words and music, is material which children can really enjoy singing. Moreover, along with the song material, the book contains many suggestions about helping children to experience music more fully, freely, and happily through bodily movement and the use of simple homemade or school-made instruments. What was happening in Miss T.'s room was very different from what one often sees in a classroom—where a song is made into a kind of lesson, with much drill on right notes and voice production, and some children are classified as "non-singers." Evidently Miss T.'s idea was that the most important single thing about music is that children shall enjoy it. That, too, is one of the central ideas of this book.)

Quickly the song ended. Instantly there was a clamor for more, and numerous eager suggestions. Smilingly Miss T. looked here and there. Finally her glance came to rest on a little girl who was standing shyly in the background.

"Is there any song you'd like us to sing, Jean dear?" she asked.

Jean's whisper was so low that I couldn't hear the words, but Miss T. caught them, all right.

"Jean would like *Knock Along, Brother Rabbit*. How would that be?" she said, addressing the group.

"Yes! Yes! Yes!" the answer came in chorus.

Another high grade for Miss T., thought I. She's using music to bring out and encourage a diffident child. How often a skillful teacher can use music to reach individual children—the diffident, the timid, the surly, the aggressive—each with his own peculiarities and problems. Here was just one actual instance. (And then I thought that our book must contain material that will help teachers to use music in such ways, material well varied and related to many human situations that appeal to children.)

I was a little surprised at the choice of the song. It was a good deal longer than the songs some people think suitable for children of pre-school age. Simple, of course, but the sort of song that older people also might enjoy singing. This brings up another point in which Miss T.'s procedures were in line with our plans for this book. Many of the songs subsequently chosen are certainly longer than those often used with very young children. Some, of course, are intended for the teacher to sing to the children. Critics might question such choices, but evidently Miss T.'s children had never been told that music as long as this was "too much" for them. They evidently wanted it and enjoyed it.

For Jean's song went very well. I should mention that Miss T. used the phonograph in leading it. The song was on a record. She played the record on the phonograph, and the children seemed to find it perfectly natural to sing along. They sang without any constraint or hesitation. And Miss T. herself was able to sing along as a member of the group, instead of playing the piano with her back turned, or perhaps leading the singing herself and

*Her children enjoy music experiences fully, freely, happily*

*Miss T.'s children call for longer songs and seem able to sing them*

viii

doing so perhaps less well than was possible with the record. (Many of the songs in this book are available in recorded form, since it has been found that children learn them easily from the records, and will sing them in a most satisfying way.)

When this second song was finished, Miss T. took over before there could be any urgent requests for still more. Very smoothly she switched the attention of the children to other things by starting to tell them a story. Aha, I thought, who said there was no special music period here? *This* was the music period, and I arrived just in time for it. But I was wrong, and before my visit ended I realized what Miss T. had really been doing.

My first hint came about twenty minutes later. Some of the children were beginning to squirm and become restless. Miss T. at once used music to deal with this human problem. There had been some talk to and fro about a circus that had recently been to town, and various animals had been mentioned.

Suddenly Miss T. said, "Let's see if we can find some music that tells how elephants walk."

Sure enough, a piece was found and everyone for the time being became elephants. Then there was a switch over to other animals. After a few minutes of this, the restlessness was all worked off.

My mind went back at once to those two songs that had greeted my arrival. They had seemed to add up to a stated music period, but Miss T. had been using them for a human purpose, just as she had used the animal music later on. At the opening of school she had wanted to give everyone a lift, to pull everything together, to start things out right; and she had used music to do it. Later on she wanted to deal with the natural restlessness of little children, and again she had used music to do it. If you want to use music "undiluted," as Miss T. did at first, you will find plenty of material in this book which is very well suited to such a purpose. If you want to use music in connection with some other activity or interest, this book contains much material that will be helpful.

When the group was dismissed I waited until everyone had left and then I introduced myself to Miss T. I told her how much I'd enjoyed my visit and congratulated her on her work.

"You must be quite a musician," I said.

"Oh no, indeed I'm not," she replied. "I've just picked things up here and there and found out what seems to work. I'm always on the lookout for ideas and material."

I mentioned our projected book to Miss T., telling her that it was to be designed very definitely for teachers who realize, as she does, how much music can do for children, and who don't have much musical training.

"What we really want to use in our book are ideas that have been tested in the classroom. May I come to see you again? I think you are working along the lines in which we are interested."

On my way out I stopped at the principal's office to tell her how much I had enjoyed my visit. She did not seem too much surprised.

"Miss T. is a fine human being," she said. I had been thinking along musical lines and I suppose I looked a bit startled at this.

*Movement with music enlivens talk about the visit of a circus*

*It is discovered that Miss T. has not had special music training*

"We try to put the person first, throughout our school," she explained. "Right down to each little individual entering our pre-school."

Then she showed me the files of Growth and Development records, one for every child in the school, kept up by the teachers of each succeeding grade the child attended.

"It is here you will find just what Miss T. has done for our children, throughout the years, by giving them such a fine start. As for music, it seems to be a wonderful factor in orienting the child, in making him feel at home in the school."

"What did you think of Miss T.?" my host asked me at the dinner table that night. There was a hush as his children searched my face, eagerly awaiting my answer.

"There seems to be unusual interest here," I said, parrying the question. "Did all you children go to school to Miss T.?"

"All except Sally." The elder daughter hung her head. Evidently her condition was a sad one.

"We just love Miss T.," one of them said.

"Yes," said my host, "there's never any trouble around here getting the chores done, so that mother can get off to school, now and then, and help in the kindergarten."

So . . . parent cooperation, too . . . that was how Miss T. worked it. This business of Miss T. was well worth looking into further. . . .

JAMES L. MURSELL
*Teachers College, Columbia University*

FOOTNOTES:

On the text pages that introduce each chapter, references are made to the following publications, each indicated by the same number, whenever cited.

1. "Guiding the Young Child," prepared by a committee of the California School Supervisors Association. Boston: D. C. Heath and Company, 1951.
2. "Music of Young Children: I. Chant," Pillsbury Foundation Study. Santa Barbara, Cal.: Pillsbury Foundation for Advancement of Music Education, 1941.
3. "Music of Young Children: II. General Observations," Pillsbury Foundation Study, 1942.
4. "Music and Movement," by Ann Driver. London: Oxford University Press, 1936.
5. "Music of Young Children: IV. Free Use of Instruments for Musical Growth," Pillsbury Foundation Study, 1951.
6. "There's Music in Children," by Emma Dickson Sheehy. New York: Henry Holt and Company, 1946.

PHOTOGRAPHS:

The faces of actual children are important to a book based on children and the reality of their needs. We are most grateful for the cooperation of the following schools in supplying photographs: Scarsdale, N. Y.,—Greenacres, p. i, Edgewood, p. 1 (public schools); Harriet Johnson Nursery School, Bank St., New York, N. Y., pgs. 21 and 77; Whiteley Nursery School, Scarsdale, N. Y., p. 95. Pictures on pgs. 35, 67, and 83, of Beachbrook Nursery School, a non-profit cooperative for children, Brooklyn, N. Y., are used by courtesy of Peripole Products, Inc., manufacturers of rhythm band instruments.

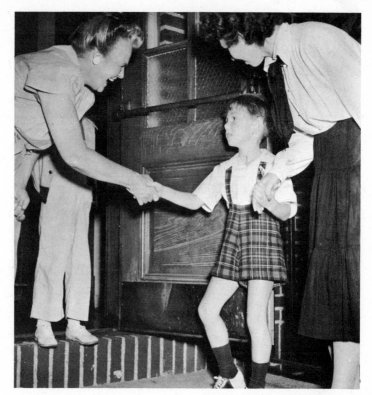

## CHAPTER ONE

Courtesy John Gass

# OUR LITTLE PEOPLE

## KEEPING SCHOOL WHOLE

"School"—what a delightful word for our little people, most of whom look forward eagerly to the time when they will be part of that mysterious world from which older children bring tales of wonder.

The child sees the school as a whole. He wants to be part of it—all of it. The principal is *his* principal, the custodian *his* custodian. All too soon he will be caught in the compartmentalization that is being so slowly shaken apart by our schools. During these first years, he goes on trips through his school with a proprietary air; thinks it only natural that his group should call, one day, upon the principal. When high school instrumentalists come to his room to demonstrate for him how their instruments should sound, he proudly shows his array of instruments to them in return.

In his own classroom he is provided with a program that stimulates his curiosity, increases his knowledge, and helps him to organize his thinking.[1] Much of this takes the form of play, for play is the child's way of thinking and reaching understanding. Musical play will be among the ways provided for the young child to relive the activities he experiences every day. Music can help the teacher provide maximum physical development, too, through rhythms. Music also contributes to emotional adjustments, encourages esthetic expression. But all this is inseparable from the children's other learnings occurring at the same time, and following the same pattern of development.

Off to school! Our little people leave home and the security and affection claimed there as a right. They come to school, where each must learn to meet the demands of his group, to adjust to the democratic pattern as a whole.

How each child meets this challenge depends on the child himself. Each child that comes to us is a unique entity, with background, needs, desires, and problems all his own. This is shown the first day. Jean evidences a predisposition to caution by clinging to her mother's skirts. Tom, an aggressive type, makes a beeline for the train in the corner, before some other child can claim it. Barbara responds easily to the teacher's smile and suggestion, and is soon playing pleasantly with a new friend.[1]

Jean, Tom, and Barbara will develop, each in his own way; they will learn much, but will continue to be different. Music can play a large part in the development of each. Just how, can be judged best by the classroom teacher, who from day to day will observe and guide this development.

1

# Sing-Song

WORDS BY MAY JUSTUS
MUSIC BY ZILPHIA HORTON

*Here they are—babies but yesterday—now grown into little people, brimful of energy and bursting with song.*

1. Some like the coun-try, Some like the town,
2. Some like a sto-ry, Some like a song,

Some trav-el up-hill, Some trav-el down.
Some march to mu-sic, Some plod a - long.

Some sing for sil-ver, Some sing for bread;
Bank - ers have mon-ey, Beg-gars have none;

I sing to let the tunes out of my head!
I have a pen-ny and plen-ty of fun!

*They like to hear "teacher" sing, too, if the tune is one they can ride along on, by using repeated words or syllables, like these "ningin's."*

# Singing School

AMERICAN FOLK SONG FROM KANSAS

Some think there's no-thing half so good as oy-sters roast-ed fried or stewed; While oth-ers say there's pleas-ure more in slid-ing down the cel-lar door. And some thinks this and some thinks that; But all a-gree there's great-er sat-is-fac-tion to be al-ways had at sing-ing school, as I have said. Oh the

G           C           A           D

1. sing - in', 'ning - in', 'ning - in', Oh the     sing - in', 'ning - in', 'ning - in', Oh the
2. sing - in', 'ning - in', 'ning - in', Oh the     sing - in', 'ning - in', 'ning - in', Of the

G           D           A           G

sing - in', 'ning - in', 'ning - in', 'ning - in',
sing - in', 'ning - in', 'ning - in', 'ning - in', 'ning - in', 'ning - in', 'ning - in'; Oh the    school.

## The Moon's Lullaby

WORDS BY KATE COX GODDARD
MUSIC BY OSBOURNE WM. McCONATHY

*Their imaginations are still unbounded and dramatic. They speak easily of "flying to the moon." Why, then, shouldn't the moon hear what they are saying, far below.*

♩=80

1. Cats howl so high,      Dogs bark so loud,      Old Man Moon just
2. Moth - er sings low,      Dad - dy sings deep,      Old Man Moon pre -

sits on a cloud And list - ens and list - ens.
tends he's a - sleep And             list - ens and list - ens.

4

*They love fun, and will be delighted to discover
that this chicken grew so tall it bumped right into
the music and broke the lines apart.*

# Shanghai Chicken

AMERICAN FOLK SONG

1. Shang-hai chick-en grows so tall; Few days; Few days; Al-most reach the
2. Great big fish they call a whale; Few days; Few days; Swal-lowed Jo-nah

top of the wall, And I'm go-in' home.
head and tail, And I'm go-in' home.
I have a home o-ver yon-der;

Few days; Few days;
I have a

home o-ver yon-der,
And I'm go-in' home.

5

# The Snowman

WORDS BY RHODA NEWTON

MUSIC BY RHODA REICHART

*They have yet to acquire many aspects of language; but they can see the joke about this snowman, who "ran away" when the weather got too warm for him.*

To make a snow-man is such fun, He has no legs to help him run, But when the sun shines warm and still, The snow-man hur-ries down the hill.

# The Woodpecker

WORDS BY MARY BLATT KOCH

MUSIC BY MARY JARMAN NELSON

*Our little people are just emerging from a very self-centered world. The woodpecker taps for them. They love to imitate his tap with their wood blocks, while they sing this song.*

Tap-a-tap-a-tap, Tap-a-tap-a-tap, What can that be?

Tap-a-tap-a-tap, Tap-a-tap-a-tap, It's a wood-peck-er in the tree!

*When the wind blows, it blows for them, does something they wish. Of course, they ask for some sunshine, so they can go outdoors to play.*

# Little Wind

WORDS BY KATE GREENAWAY
MUSIC BY LILLIAN BALDWIN

Lit - tle wind, blow on the hill - top, Lit - tle wind, blow down the plain. Lit - tle wind, blow up the sun-shine, Lit - tle wind, blow off the rain!

*Their world is "here and now." A year is too long for them to measure; but changing seasons are anticipated because they bring "my new birthday."*

# April

WORDS AND MUSIC BY GRACE R. BURLIN

Says the rob - in, in the spring-time, "I think it will rain. But __ soon __ the __ sun will be shin - ing a - gain."

7

# Dancing Stars

WORDS BY VERNETTA DECKER
MUSIC BY MABEL E. BRAY

*Contrasting with this practical concern for that which can be experienced at the moment, our little people are endlessly fascinated by the mystery of the bright stars above.*

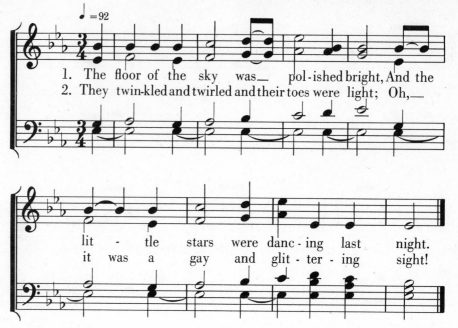

1. The floor of the sky was pol-ished bright, And the
2. They twin-kled and twirled and their toes were light; Oh,—

lit - tle stars were danc-ing last night.
it was a gay and glit-ter-ing sight!

# Counting Song

WORDS BY MAY JUSTUS
MUSIC BY ZILPHIA HORTON

*They love numbers, too, and feel big when they are counting. They are also developing a strong sense of family and home.*

1. One, two, three, One, two, three, How man-y peo-ple are one, two, three?
2. Just one more, Just one more, How man-y peo-ple are just one more?

One, two, three, One, two, three, Moth - er and Dad-dy and I make three.
Just one more, Just one more, That is the ba - by and that makes four.

*On one nature trip, Jane found a baby bird on the sidewalk. "Poor little bird, it is lost from its home." The children would not move until the custodian came to put the fledgling back into its nest.*

# Little Redbird in the Tree

AMERICAN FOLK SONG—GEORGIA VERSION

♩=96

1. Lit-tle red-bird in the tree, in the tree, in the tree, Lit-tle red-bird
2. Lit-tle snow-bird in the tree, in the tree, in the tree, Lit-tle snow-bird

in the tree, sing a song to me. *Fine* Sing a-bout the ros - es
in the tree, sing a song to me. Sing a-bout the cloud - land

*D.C. al Fine*

On the gar-den wall. Sing a-bout the bird swings In the tree-top tall.
Way up in the sky. When you go there call - ing, Do your bird-ies cry?

3. Little bluebird in the tree,
   In the tree, in the tree,
   Little bluebird in the tree,
   Sing a song to me.

   Sing about the mountains,
   Lovely they must be.
   Sing about the steamboats
   Out there on the sea.

4. Little blackbird in the tree, etc.

   Sing about the farmer
   Planting peas and beans.
   Sing about the harvest,
   I know what that means.

## Dance to Your Daddy

WORDS FROM MOTHER GOOSE
MUSIC BY ELSA CROSS

*Our little people are deeply rooted in the security of home, but daddy and mother are becoming more than mere providers of what is wanted.*

Dance to your dad-dy, my lit-tle ba-by, Dance to your dad-dy,

my lit-tle lamb; You shall have a fish-ie, in a lit-tle dish-ie,

You shall have a fish-ie when the boat comes in.

## Philippine Lullaby

BASED ON AN APAYAO FOLK SONG

*At bedtime they may still enjoy being cuddled like babies and sung, if not rocked, to sleep.*

Up-on a moun-tain far a-way,     A moth-er sings so soft and low:
"My lit-tle ba-by, go to sleep;     My lit-tle ba-by, go to sleep."

10

*But in broad daylight, mother and father are often cast for the role of hero or heroine of the tales they tell to their fellows, while at play.*

# Now Sleep Gently

NORWEGIAN FOLK SONG

Now sleep gen-tly lit - tle one, ma - ma will come back a - gain. Pa - pa's gone in - to the town, gone to buy you brand new shoes. Bright new shoes with buck - les too; so, sleep lit-tle one, go to sleep my dear.

Children accept home and all favors received there as their natural right. Little by little, they are led to see that home life also entails responsibilities. Schools that carry on a Family Living program like to acquaint their preschoolers with roles that they can usefully play at home, as part of the play in the Doll House. Miss T.'s children have a "Housecleaning Song":

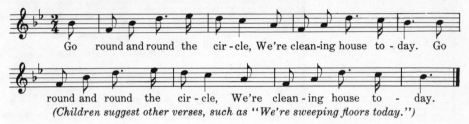

Go round and round the cir-cle, We're clean-ing house to-day. Go

round and round the cir-cle, We're clean-ing house to-day.

*(Children suggest other verses, such as "We're sweeping floors today.")*

The children move busily about the Doll House. Here is a song called "Setting the Table," that makes it fun to help mother at dinner time.

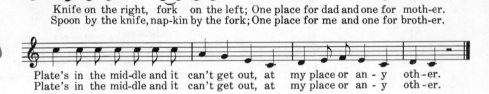

Knife on the right, fork on the left; One place for dad and one for moth-er.
Spoon by the knife, nap-kin by the fork; One place for me and one for broth-er.

Plate's in the mid-dle and it can't get out, at my place or an-y oth-er.
Plate's in the mid-dle and it can't get out, at my place or an-y oth-er.

## Dolly's Lullaby

*Each child is too busy with his responsibilities to sing, excepting Marjorie, who sits in the corner rocking her "little sister" to sleep.*

CANON BY TEN-YEAR-OLD CHILD

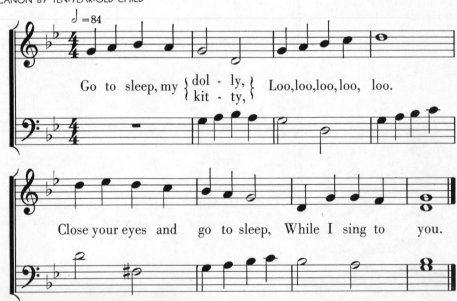

Go to sleep, my { dol - ly, / kit - ty, } Loo, loo, loo, loo, loo.

Close your eyes and go to sleep, While I sing to you.

The children have been helped to understand that mother has more time to grant them personal favors when her family cooperates. Today, daddy and all the children have been model family members and Barbara, the "mother," who sings quite well, decides to sing them a story as a reward.

12

*Miss T. smiles to herself when she hears the song that Barbara has chosen, and finds consolation in the thought that Family Living is stressed at every level, in her school.*

# Oh, Daddy Be Gay

AMERICAN FOLK SONG

♩. = 80

1. There was an old wo-man lived un-der the hill,
2. One day she sent her old man___ to plow,

Oh, Dad-dy be gay!___ There was an old wo-man lived
Oh, Dad-dy be gay!___ One day she sent her old

un-der the hill, If she had-n't moved out she'd be
man___ to plow, And when he ___ got there, he

liv-ing there still. So, Dad-dy be gay and eat can-dy!
did-n't know how. So, Dad-dy be gay and eat can-dy!

3.  So he went out to the kitch—en door,
    Oh, Daddy be gay!
    So he went out to the kitch—en door,
    And he said — "I've eaten but I want some more."
    So, Daddy be gay and eat candy!

4.  And so she gave him some bread — and meat,
    Oh, Daddy be gay!
    And so she gave him some bread — and meat,
    And when he — had eaten he danced down the street.
    So, Daddy be gay and eat candy!

25

# Who's That Knocking at My Door?

AMERICAN FOLK SONG

*One way to help at home is by answering the bell and greeting guests nicely. This little chore assumes more importance if it is practiced at school.*

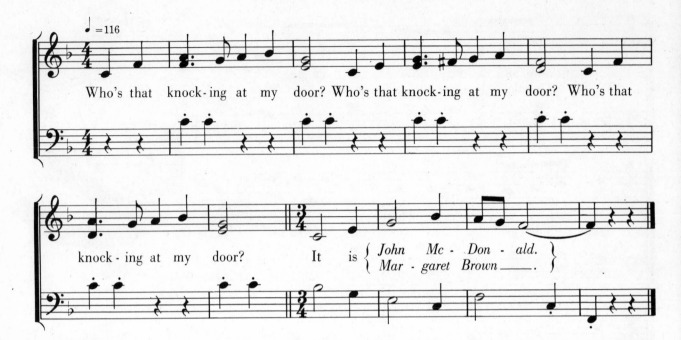

Who's that knock-ing at my door? Who's that knock-ing at my door? Who's that knock-ing at my door? It is { John Mc-Don-ald. Mar-garet Brown_____. }

2. I will hurry to my door
   *(3 times)*
   And say, "How do you do?"
   *(Or "Hello, Tommy." Children choose*
   *appropriate phrase.)*

3. I will shake his hand
   *(3 times)*
   And say, "Please come in."
   *(Or any other phrase children decide upon.)*

4. I will lead him to a chair
   *(3 times)*
   And say, "Do sit down."

*Children stand still in a circle as they sing. One child is the "visitor" who runs around outside the circle, pausing to knock at the door (on the floor) behind one of the children in the circle. This child then acts out the words of the song, inviting his guest to come inside the circle and sit down on one of the chairs that have been placed there. At the close of the song the "visitor" takes the place of the "host" in the circle, while the "host" has a turn at being visitor.*

Robin is a shy, sensitive child who needs help in developing natural relationships with the members of his group. One day the girls in the Doll House were too busy with their dolls to hear his polite knock on the door. Noticing his hurt expression, Miss T. quickly sang, "Who's that knocking at my door?" There was a scurrying inside, and the door quickly opened to the sung phrase, "It is Robin Jackson."

14

# Moon's Eye View

WORDS AND MUSIC BY LILLIAN CROWELL

*We recognize each child as an individual, contriving a stanza for each of our children. These stanzas are sung in proper turn, or at special times.*

The Man in the Moon looked down one night, And I saw him wink in the pale moon-light; I heard him say to a lit-tle star, "I'm glad that we can see so far."

2. "When Sally lifts her lovely eyes,
   And speaks her thoughts so young and wise,
   I'm sure that we shall never hear
   A voice so soft and sweet and clear."

3. "Now I love girls, but there's one boy,
   A fine young chap whose name is Roy;
   If he makes a wish when I am new,
   I'll try to see that it comes true."

4. "I love the kids of every land,
   But somehow these seem extra grand;
   So I'll throw them some soft moon-beams,
   And wish all of them 'Happy Dreams.'"

15

## I Have A Bonnet Trimmed with Blue

ENGLISH SINGING GAME

*"Mary has a new dress that is blue," "Tommy has a cap with a tassel on,"—how easy to draw an admiring circle around a child, recognizing him and the pride he takes in wearing new clothes.*

I have a bon-net trimmed with blue! Why don't you wear it? So I do!

When do you wear it? When I can! When I go out with my young man!

## Selling Song

ADAPTED FROM AN OLD CHANT

*A child may have something to sell. He calls his wares, using this chant which is reminiscent of the street cries of earlier times.*

1. Ap-ples ripe! Ap-ples ripe! Who will buy my ap-ples ripe?
2. Good hot cakes! Good hot cakes! Who will buy my good hot cakes?

## The Riddle

ANNA MARY MEALAND

*Or some child comes to you in the morning bearing a "treasure." You can add so much to his pleasure and sense of importance by letting him make a singing riddle of it.*

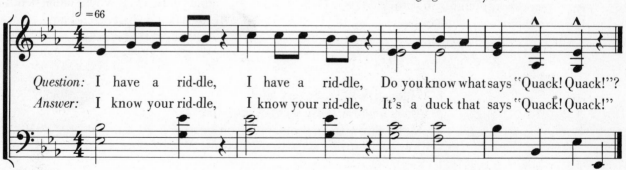

*Question:* I have a rid-dle, I have a rid-dle, Do you know what says "Quack! Quack!"?
*Answer:* I know your rid-dle, I know your rid-dle, It's a duck that says "Quack! Quack!"

16

*Since the individual is but one member of the group, there are lessons in social living. Kings bow low to their queens; today's gentlemen tip their hats to the ladies.*

# Lavender's Blue

ENGLISH FOLK SONG

♪=120

Lav-en-der's blue, dil-ly dal-ly, Lav-en-der's green;

When I am king, dil-ly dal-ly, You shall be queen.

*And practice in passing refreshments without spilling comes in handy both at school and at home, when company comes.*

# Cookies

WORDS BY MAY JUSTUS
MUSIC BY ZILPHIA HORTON

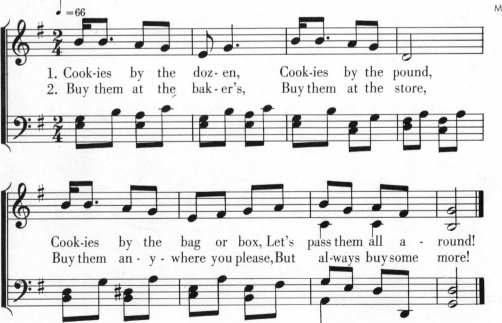

♩=66

1. Cook-ies by the doz-en, Cook-ies by the pound,
2. Buy them at the bak-er's, Buy them at the store,

Cook-ies by the bag or box, Let's pass them all a-round!
Buy them an-y-where you please, But al-ways buy some more!

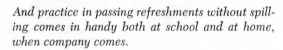

17

# Mister Policeman

WORDS BY MARION K. SEAVEY
MUSIC BY GERTRUDE E. McGUNIGLE

*But home is not quite enough for the pre-schooler. Our little people are now ready for community experiences. We take them on trips through town.*

Mis-ter Po-lice-man, how do you do? Please, may I go a-long with you?

You stop the cars to let me through, Please, may I cross the street with you?

# Mister Barber

WORDS AND MUSIC BY MARY BLATT KOCH

Mis-ter Bar-ber, cut my hair, While I sit in your great big chair;

Snip a lit-tle here, Snip a lit-tle there, Mis-ter Bar-ber, cut my hair.

18

*The policeman helps us across the street. We may visit the firehouse and talk about the need for firemen, who are always ready to save our homes from fire.*

# Playing Fireman

WORDS BY ELEANOR GRAHAM VANCE
MUSIC BY MARION BAUER

Bong! Bong! Bong! Bong! Where's the fire? Where's the fire? Bong! Bong! Bong! Bong!

Start the truck! Start the truck! Bong! Bong! Bong! Bong! Squirt the hose! Squirt the hose!

Bong! Bong! Bong! Bong! Put the fire out! Put the fire out!

*Out of discussions like these grows respect for all members of the community who serve the home,— the barber, the milkman, the grocery boy.*

# Community Helpers

WORDS AND MUSIC BY ELIZABETH GRENOBLE

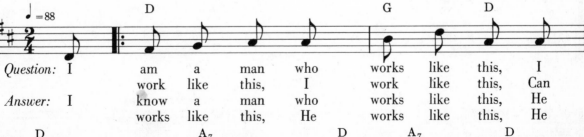

*Question:* I am a man who works like this, I
work like this, I work like this, Can

*Answer:* I know a man who works like this, He
works like this, He works like this, He

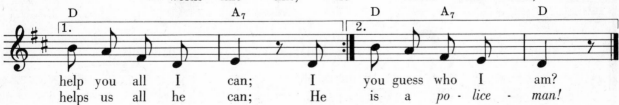

help you all I can; I you guess who I am?
helps us all he can; He is a po - lice - man!

# The Shoemaker

ENGLISH FOLK SONG
FROM THE SOUTHERN APPALACHIANS

*Here's an old, old song about a cobbler. Your children will like to use instruments to hammer out the rhythm they heard in the shoe repair shop.*

I am a shoe - mak-er by my trade, I'll work in rain - y weath - er; Be-sides, two pair I've made to - day, Of a side and a half of leath-er. Whack de loo de dum, whack de loo de doo-dy, whack de loo de dum; Kate, you are my dar - ling.

20

## CHAPTER TWO

## WHEN IS MUSIC TIME?

How can we fence in a child's music between the hands of a clock? Music is movement. The child moves all the day long. His kind of music is part of every waking moment, since his time is spent in almost constant activity. The sound of a stick run across the radiator is music to his ears. He not only hammers; he is aware of and pleased with the rhythm he makes while hammering.

This pleasure he expresses in song— the songs he makes, himself . . . "Some sung to himself, alone, quietly, of everyday things, as though the melody, not the words, was important." More frequently these songs are "rhythmic, like a ritual chant; the voice clings to one note around which it weaves a melodic pattern limited and insistent in form."[2]

A group takes down building blocks from the shelf, pushing them across the floor. The movement happens to fall into a rhythm pattern and "chant" results.

"To produce his own music a young child's first need is freedom—freedom to move about in pursuit of his own interests and purposes, and freedom to make the sounds appropriate to them."[3] Miss T. says, "If only I remember to listen and not to talk, I hear music all day long."

Children enjoy a time set aside for music; but that time is when the moment is ripe. Music is never "precious," something "special." Play is enhanced by music and music by play. Even the words of a song are more easily learned if the song is taught in a child's real-life situation.

*Courtesy Werner Wolff*

# MUSIC ALL DAY

Miss T. was in the middle of an entrancing story when the window washer opened the door and clattered in.

"And the little train said—" Bang, bang went the window washer's pails. Every face in the circle showed disappointment. What had the train said? They couldn't hear it.

Slosh! slosh! went the big rubber boots over the floor, as the man went tramp! tramp! to the sink to draw water.

"Let's make the sound of the window washer's boots on the floor," said Miss T., closing the book. With their hands, they "tramp-tramped" in rhythm with the big boots as the man sloshed back and forth across the room.

"Let's watch him, now, and sing what he does." Johnny sang:                          Sara sang:

He's wash-ing the wind-ows.              He's wip - ing them dry.—

When the man had finished, a contrasting phrase was added, and a new song was ready to add to their repertory.

## Our Windshield Wiper

WORDS BY LUCY M. HARRISON
MUSIC BY WINIFRED HARRISON CRISS

*Our little people are spread out all over the floor, busy with individual or group block building projects. It is raining outdoors. John remembers this song and decides to start the wiper on his "auto."*

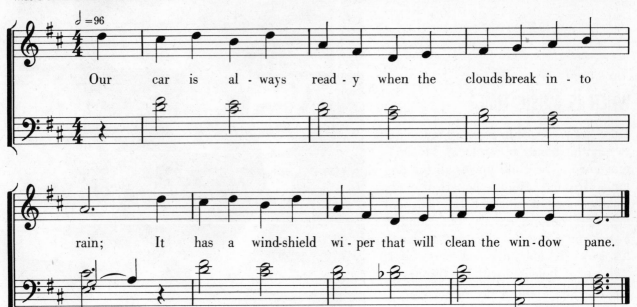

Our car is al-ways read-y when the clouds break in-to

rain; It has a wind-shield wi-per that will clean the win-dow pane.

## Here Comes the Train

*Tony puts the last block on his train. "The caboose is ready," he calls. "All aboard." "Do we need tickets?" one child asks.*

WORDS AND MUSIC BY ELSIE-JEAN

Here comes the train, Have you bought your tick - et?

I have mine, I have mine, I have mine, All a-board.

"Have you got your tickets?" sings Miss T. The group picks up the phrase at once, since it enhances their play. In a moment the song is learned. If enough of her group drop their play and come together, Miss T. may decide that this is the best time of the day to have music time. Other train songs may be sung. Her children like to choose instruments that add reality to their activity. They discover sand blocks useful for a "choo-choo" sound.

22

*This song came in handy, one day, when Tom, who is very aggressive, insisted that he alone must be the whistle on the train he had built. In the song, of course, they all took turns.*

# Let's Take a Little Trip

WORDS AND MUSIC BY LOLLY WILLIAMS

♩=108

1. Let's take a lit-tle trip. Shall we board a train? We will trav-el
2. Let's take a lit-tle trip. Would you like to fly? We will take an

miles and miles    O-ver hill and    plain.    Woo! Woo! The whis-tle blows,
aer-o-plane;    See the clouds go    by.    Up! Up! In-to the air.

Woo!    Woo!    A-way!    Good-bye! Good-bye! We'll be back some    day.
Up!    Up!    A-way!

# Busy Trucks

WORDS AND MUSIC BY EVA A. SANDERSON

*All sorts of trucks are built of blocks. And by changing a word here and there, such songs take us anywhere that we would like to go.*

Sand trucks, grav-el trucks, Big old ce-ment trucks,

Build me a road, A road to the sea; So I can ride a-long,

ride a-long, ride a-long, And jump in-to the o-cean, One, Two, Three! Whee!
*(spoken)*

*accel.*

*glissando*

24

*Or perhaps it is a boat that draws the children together with excitement. Delight in both boat and song is increased if a song is taught then.*

# The Allee Allee O!

SINGING FOLK GAME FROM MASSACHUSETTS

Oh, the big ship's a-sail-ing through the Al-lee Al-lee O, the Al-lee Al-lee O, the Al-lee Al-lee O! Oh, the big ship's a-sail-ing through the Al-lee Al-lee O! Hi! Ding-dong-day!

One day Tom and Peter were arguing over who was to be captain of the boat which they had built cooperatively. Block time was about over, so Miss T. decided to step in. "Three times around," she sang, gathering both boys into the group that came running to join this favorite English circle game,—"The Gallant Ship."

*(collected and arranged by Cecil J. Sharp)*

Three times a-round went our gal-lant ship, And three times a-round went she, And three times a-round went our gal-lant ship, And we sink to the bot-tom of the sea.

By permission of Novello & Co., Ltd.

As the children bobbed low, both quarrel and boat "sank to the bottom of the sea," and the children were ready for a new activity. But first the blocks had to be put away neatly. Since singing makes such chores pleasanter, Miss T.'s group has a song, adapted to "The Muffin Man" tune:

Oh, do you know what time it is, what time it is, what time it is? Oh, do you know what time it is? It's time to put a-way.

When directions are sung by the teacher, her chores are easier, too. Miss T. often offers both a hand and a tune to help move a lagging child along:

Rose, Rose and up she ris-es,
*(See full song, page 32)*

Sometimes her signals are given at the piano—sometimes on an instrument in which she hopes the children will become interested. Children often help, by joining in the American folk song, "Here we go Zudio":

Oh, here we go Zu-di-o, Zu-di-o, Zu-di-o. Here we go Zu-di-o all day long.

Or the teacher may make a game of it, knowing that her children love riddles. Miss T. uses the tune of "The Pawpaw Patch":

Where, oh where is pret-ty lit-tle El - lie? Where, oh where is
pret - ty lit - tle El - lie? Where, oh where is
pret - ty lit - tle El - lie? She's o - ver in the doll cor - ner.

*This song may be sung over and over, while the children are waiting for the bus, or for parents to come to take them home.*

## Good-bye Song

CZECH FOLK SONG

Now we must all go home. Tell me good - bye, and I'll
tell you good - bye, and then we will all go home.

*There are quiet songs, too, which slow down the day's movements, as the children drop their play and get ready to take their rest.*

## Rest Song

ADAPTED FROM A FINNISH FOLK SONG

Of all the things we like to do, Those we like the best
Some-how seem more fun to do when we've had our rest.

# The Stars and Me

WORDS BY RAYMOND ABRASHKIN
MUSIC BY PETER GORDON

*As teacher sings quietly, the shades are drawn, blankets are pulled up over relaxed bodies, and weary eyelids close.*

When night comes o-ver the prai-rie,— Down to sleep I lie,—

Un-der my own lit-tle blan-ket,— Gaz-ing at the sky.— High

up a-bove, The stars I see. They're all I have for— com-pa-ny. Then

close our eyes, And go to sleep. Me and the stars, The— stars and me.

See record 716, "The Little Cowboy."

*But soon it's time to "knock along" again. "I asked him where was he goin'." "Says, goin' to the playground." Many uses are found for this song.*

# Knock Along Brother Rabbit

AMERICAN FOLK SONG

29

After rest time comes outdoor play. Singing games are particularly useful when, occasionally, organized play is desirable. They are useful, too, on rainy days, when the children cannot go out-of-doors. The social aspect of these games also makes them valuable. A child's schoolmates are very important to him at this age; he must make a place for himself in the group. In a circle game every individual is accepted, is equally important. There is comfort in the clasp of hands as our little people sing merrily and swing around a circle.

## Two in the Middle

*Round and round to this tune, which is sparked by the added fun of numbers and counting.*

AMERICAN FOLK GAME (ADAPTED)

Two in the mid-dle and they can't get out,— Two in the mid-dle and they can't get out,— Two in the mid-dle and they can't get out!— Oh my lil-lee O!

2. Swing you another, and another one in,
   Swing you another, and another one in,
   Swing you another, and another one in,
   Oh my lillee O!

Three in the middle, then swing you another; then four in the middle, then swing another in, etc., ending with "Ten (or another number) do-si and jump for joy, Oh my lillee O!"

*Paul was better liked by his fellows when they discovered how well he could "leap and hop," when called on by Miss T. to play the leading role in this game.*

# Lily, Lily Wallflowers

ENGLISH CIRCLE GAME

Li - ly, li - ly wall-flowers, grow-ing up the wall; We are all child - ren,

grow-ing up so tall. Look at { Sal - ly Tay - lor and { she's the best of all; { Ken-neth Jud - son } { he's

{ She } can hop and { she } can skip and { she } can jump the can-dle stick; Heigh ho! What a trick.
{ He } { he } { he }

1, 2, 3, etc.
Turn your back to the wall a - gain.

last ending
Turn your back to the wall a - gain.

Why do children like some of their fellows better than others? Usually the reasons are easy to understand; but even a discerning teacher has some-times been surprised at the results shown on a carefully plotted sociogram. By recording children's free choices of partners, she discovers some child is left out—is an "isolate." She may not at once know why; but her sociogram tells her she must find a way to help this child draw closer into the circle. She will approach the problem of the sensitive, maladjusted child with great care. Sometimes, however, encouragement is all that is needed.

31

# Drop the Handkerchief

GERMAN SINGING GAME

*Sometimes the game has been invented to fit the song. Sometimes the game, like this one that is well-loved, has created the music.*

A-round the cir-cle, while I run, The hand-ker-chief will find you, will find you. Now

your turn comes to share the fun. I've dropped it! Look be-hind you, be-hind you.

# Rose, Rose and Up She Rises

NURSERY SONG FROM THE APPALACHIANS
COLLECTED AND ARRANGED BY CECIL J. SHARP

*Here is a choosing game that helps a teacher discover which of her children are "stars" and which tend to be "isolates." The latter, once discovered, are chosen to begin the game.*

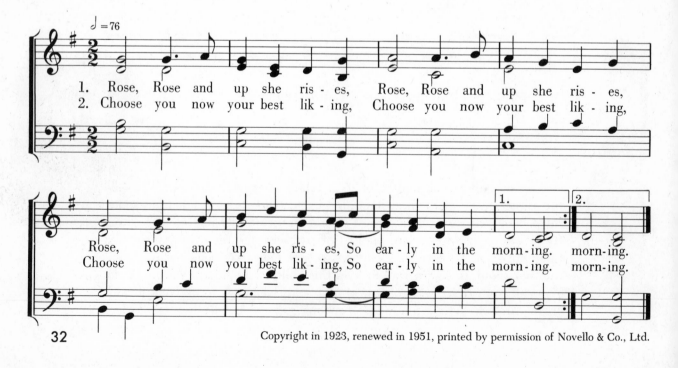

1. Rose, Rose and up she ris - es,   Rose, Rose and up she ris - es,
2. Choose you now your best lik - ing,   Choose you now your best lik - ing,

Rose, Rose and up she ris - es, So ear-ly in the morn-ing. morn-ing.
Choose you now your best lik - ing, So ear-ly in the morn-ing. morn-ing.

*Our little people gradually learn, through games like this, that it's important to be pleasant about the matter of taking turns.*

# Old King Glory

AMERICAN SINGING GAME

Old King Glo - ry of the val - ley! The moun-tain was so high, it

near - ly touched the sky. The first one, the sec-ond one, the third fol - low me.

*Singing games have been played and loved by children of every nationality. This little game has become traditional in America.*

# Sally Go Round the Chimney Pot

AMERICAN SINGING GAME

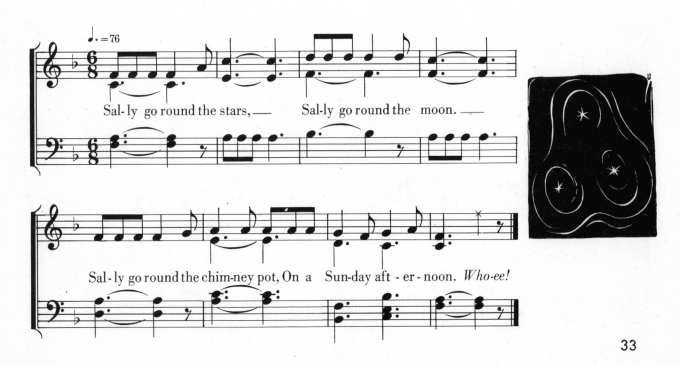

Sal - ly go round the stars, — Sal - ly go round the moon. —

Sal - ly go round the chim-ney pot, On a Sun-day aft - er - noon. *Who-ee!*

# Rudy, Rudy, Rannie

EAST EUROPEAN JEWISH PLAY SONG

*This is a favorite of long ago, in East European countries. As in all singing games, the action follows the words.*

Ru - dy, Ru - dy, Ran - nie, One for sis - ter An - nie, Two for Un - cle Har - ry,

Three for cous - in Car - rie. Three times a - round; Now we all sit down.

# Skip to My Lou

AMERICAN SINGING GAME

*Here is a favorite among American children and teachers, too, who find "Lou" versatile and adaptable to many times and places. There are hundreds of verses. Why not add a few more?*

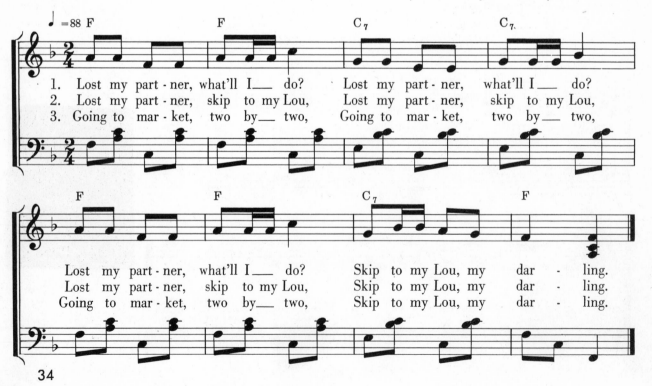

1. Lost my part - ner, what'll I __ do?   Lost my part - ner, what'll I __ do?
2. Lost my part - ner, skip to my Lou,   Lost my part - ner, skip to my Lou,
3. Going to mar - ket, two by __ two,   Going to mar - ket, two by __ two,

Lost my part - ner, what'll I __ do?   Skip to my Lou, my dar - ling.
Lost my part - ner, skip to my Lou,   Skip to my Lou, my dar - ling.
Going to mar - ket, two by __ two,   Skip to my Lou, my dar - ling.

34

## CHAPTER THREE

Courtesy Peripole Products, Inc.

## PATTERNED MOVEMENT

Freddy swings around the pole, and is delighted with the motion. As he swings, again and again, he falls into an action-pattern. He will unconsciously use this same pattern tomorrow, when he swings around the pole. On another day he may chant, "Whirly, twirly, curly, burly." It will be no accident if music occurs to him to express his joy in motion; for music has repeated patterns, too.

Fred's play is enhanced if others join him. He and a small group may hop, roll, crawl,—all delightful rhythmic experiences. Not all children hop, skip, and roll just alike. Jane skips with a light foot; Tom lunges forward with his whole body. Each moves in his own pattern, at a rate of speed comfortable to him. This is true, also, of dramatic play.[3]

"I'll be a horsey. You be a dog, Jane."

Jane gets down on all fours and after some experimentation settles into a gait used subsequently for all her "dogness."

Thus when we step in to hold the play together, we underline the child's basic pattern with drum, tambourine, or piano. We play a $\frac{2}{4}$ ♫ | ♫ for running; but at the child's speed.

There must be no forcing of pace. The child's rhythmic concepts must be untrammeled until his own rhythm is released and strengthened.[4] Then, and then only, he may become "the shadow" of another, be asked to move in the same way and at the same time another child moves. Meanwhile, within the group, a rhythmic polyphony is established and felt by the children.

# MOVING WITH MUSIC

Rhythmic bodily movement of a dramatic and joyous character is included among the daily activities in our schools. Since it not only exercises the body muscles, but also promotes motor coordination, posture, and poise, classroom teachers, working with small groups wherever possible, see that all children get these benefits.

It becomes a medium of art expression when children, free to experiment, create results that satisfy them. It is then that they use this medium for outward expression of inner feelings. They express their moods or feelings in pantomime; they reproduce real-life experiences in their dramatic play, seeking to get inside these experiences and understand them by role-playing. Thus rhythmic bodily movement sends the body into action in company with both mind and social being.[4]

All this builds a readiness for understanding what music has to say. When children have created many patterns with sound and movement, they will be ready to adapt themselves to patterns set by the music; they will hear and express both imaginative content and rhythm, as they move.

35

# Digging in the Sand

ADAPTED FROM AN OLD NURSERY SONG

*Barbara was patting one side of the giant mound in the sandpile; John, the other. When other children fell into this patting rhythm, Miss T. began singing the sandpile song, in their tempo.*

1. If we dig and we dig in the sand up-on the beach, We are lia-ble to come to the wa-ter un-der neath. If we dig and dig and dig, not as far as just one mile, We will have, I should think, e-nough sand for a sand pile.

2. If we damp-en and damp-en the sand as we dig, We can build up a sand fort that's aw-ful-ly big. If we pat and pat and pat the wet sand, as it's piled high, We can build it and build it up al-most to the sky.

The big beach umbrella had to come out of the closet as a unit, "Day at the Seashore," developed. This rhythmic activity started with a small group, but most of the children came running as "props" arrived. Miss T. drummed a running beat and suggested they run in and out of the water.

# Walking in the Sand

ADAPTED FROM A FRENCH FOLK SONG

*After a rest in the sun and a taking of turns at lying under the big umbrella, the children were ready to walk on "the beach." As they walked, their shoes got heavier and heavier with sand.*

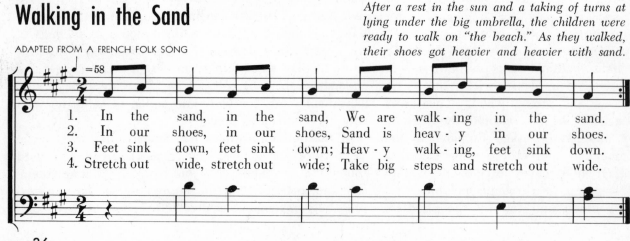

1. In the sand, in the sand, We are walk-ing in the sand.
2. In our shoes, in our shoes, Sand is heav-y in our shoes.
3. Feet sink down, feet sink down; Heav-y walk-ing, feet sink down.
4. Stretch out wide, stretch out wide; Take big steps and stretch out wide.

*Then they sang this song and pretended they were throwing shells far into the water. Robin just tossed his shells. Miss T. said they'd never reach the water. (Robin likes books better than exercise.)*

# Throwing Seashells

ADAPTED FROM A THURINGIAN FOLK SONG

Here's a lit-tle { sea-shell / star-fish } washed up by the o-cean,

See if you can throw it far a-cross the wa-ter.

37

# Skipping Merrily

FRENCH FOLK SONG

Sara skipped across the room, watching the play of shadow on her legs. Pedro skipped, too. Miss T. used the piano, instead of a tambourine; smiling encouragement at Jane whose skip was uncertain.

# Bouncing Balls

A. HILLER AND L. HOLTY

"I am the bouncer and you are the balls," said Miss T., showing with outstretched hand when the children were to take deep knee bends, as the music was played. "Now, half of you are bouncers and the other half balls." . . . "Now we'll play the music again and the bouncers will be balls, etc."

38

*Someone started a jumping play, the day it rained*
*so hard the children couldn't go outdoors. Most of*
*them joined, so boisterously that Miss T. decided*
*to transform this into a rhythmic music experience.*

# Jump, Jump, Jump

GAELIC NURSERY SONG

*When Jean, who tires easily, dropped out of the*
*game, Miss T. switched to a song in the same*
*rhythm as the jump, and sang softly to herself.*
*When the group had quieted down, she suggested*
*the children sit down, catch their breath, and sing.*

# Jump and Hop

WORDS AND MUSIC BY LENA MILAM

Jump! jump! Hop, hop, hop; Step, step, Turn a-round and stop. Face your part-ner,

Take her by the hand, Skip-pi-ty-skip! We are a hap-py band.

39

# Jungle Gym

EVA A. SANDERSON

*The day Paul climbed to the top of the jungle gym was a red letter day for Miss T., who had tried constantly to help him overcome the timidity which had been caused by over-anxious tending, at home. She called her children to sing and clap approval.*

♩ = 96

1. Watch me climb my jun-gle gym, jun-gle gym, jun-gle gym,
2. Now I am a mon-key slim, mon-key slim, mon-key slim,

*Spoken:*   8va

Watch me climb my jun-gle gym, High, high, High!
Watch me swing from limb to limb, High, high, High!

---

# Song for Swinging

ARRANGED FROM AN ALSATIAN FOLK SONG

*Jane and John stand side by side, facing front. Their arms join to make a swing. Tony pushes the swing from behind, breaking through (running under) at the climax. Another child then is pusher.*

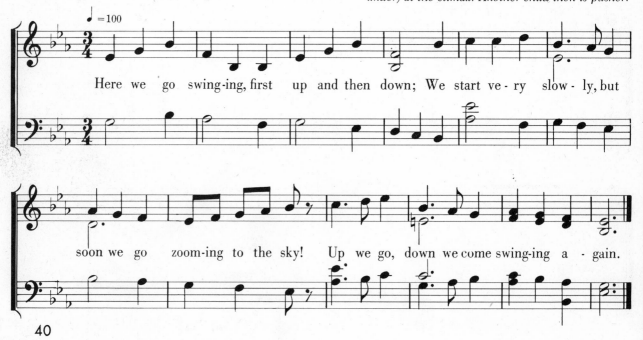

♩ = 100

Here we go swing-ing, first up and then down; We start ve-ry slow-ly, but

soon we go zoom-ing to the sky! Up we go, down we come swing-ing a - gain.

40

Miss T.'s group was busy sewing. Tempers and threads were getting snarled. "Stitch ... pull, Stitch . . . pull," sang Miss T., over and over, to a familiar chant. Transformed into a rhythmic activity, little bodies relaxed, sewing became easier, stitches evener. The sewing song was enjoyed so much that it was sung on other days, while the children only pretended to sew. Pleased with this success, Miss T. used a 2/4 chant, when hair-brushing came up in health education.

Similarly, in the autumn, leaves on the playground were raked rhythmically, to a song, with drum rolls for bending and squatting as a pile was made, loaded into a basket, and carried to the compost heap. Thus a nature lesson providing exercise for many body muscles became such a joyous thing that it continued on and on in the classroom, after the leaves had gone.

In order to practise the rhythms that make movement freer, more effective, more joyous, we must see and feel them. On one trip, the children wanted to stop and watch a man row a boat. "Back . . . pull," Miss T. repeated over and over, helping the children see that the man was rowing rhythmically. They clapped the rhythm. Back in school they made boats by sitting on the floor in pairs, facing, with soles of feet touching and both hands joined with their partners'. "Back . . . pull." They "rowed" their boats.

Rhythmic activities performed on the floor aid greatly in securing relaxation, as the fear of falling is eliminated; provide good exercise, too, as rolling, crawling, etc., involve muscles other than those used for hopping, skipping, and jumping. One day, toward the end of the rest period, Joey became restless and started to kick his heels in the air. The children turned to watch. Catching his tempo with a drum, Miss T. said, "Joey looks like a bear at a circus. Let's all bounce balls with our feet." Another day they lay on their backs and rode tricycles. They often begged for "leg music."

*It is easy to rock back and forth to music. It is easy to see the rhythm, when someone rocks in a chair. Simple experiences, like this, build a background for more complicated rhythms.*

## I Am Rocking

WORDS AND MUSIC BY MARIAN LYLE PEDEN

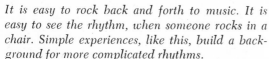
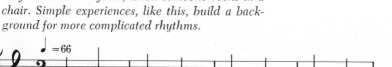
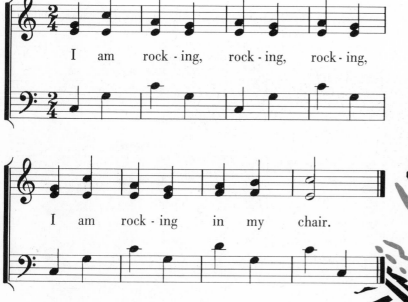

I am rock-ing, rock-ing, rock-ing,

I am rock-ing in my chair.

# The Camel

WORDS AND MUSIC BY GLADYS TIPTON

*How does a camel move? Can we imagine what it would feel like to rock back and forth on a camel's back, as he plods across desert sands? In addition to back and forth motion, would there be up and down motion, too?*

Fun-ny, hump-y cam-el, Take me for a ride.

Back and forth and back and forth, And back and forth we go.

# One Day One Foot Kept Moving

SINGING GAME FROM KANSAS

*After this and many similar experiences, Miss T. knew that her children were ready for songs with words that gave them clues to movement. She began with this simple cumulative song, which kept accumulating more and more verses, to prolong the fun.*

1. One day one foot kept mov-ing, kept mov-ing, kept mov-ing, One
2. One day one hand kept mov-ing, kept mov-ing, kept mov-ing, One
3. One day one head kept mov-ing, kept mov-ing, kept mov-ing, One

day one foot           kept mov-ing, Heigh 'O Heigh 'O. Heigh 'O.
day one foot, one hand      kept mov-ing, Heigh 'O Heigh 'O. Heigh 'O.
day one foot, one hand, one head kept mov-ing, Heigh 'O Heigh 'O. Heigh 'O.

42

# This Old Man

ENGLISH SINGING GAME

*As the children reach the last phrase of the song, Miss T. points to one child, who demonstrates how he wants the old man to come home. Pedro always chooses hopping. As the song is sung again, the children hop and sing, all about the room, converging into the original circle as the last phrase is reached. The song is resung, in the meter in which it is written. At the end, another child is asked to give a different clue for movement.*

♩ = 72

1. This old man, he played one, He played nick-nack on my drum;
2. This old man, he played two, He played nick-nack on my shoe;
3. This old man, he played three, He played nick-nack on my tree;

Nick-nack, pad-dy whack, give a dog a bone, This old man came roll-ing home.

Running

Crawling
R.H.
L.H.

Skipping

43

# Dance, Thumbkin, Dance

OLD ENGLISH

*Most large muscle exercise comes spontaneously, from the children themselves. As a contrast to vigorous activities, finger plays are found useful, occasionally. They aid small muscle coordination.*

Dance, Thumb-kin, dance! Dance, Thumb-kin, dance! Thumb-kin can-not dance a-lone, So dance my mer-ry men, ev-'ry one, And dance, Thumb-kin, dance.

# London Hill

ENGLISH NURSERY SONG

*As I was going up London Hill, I wiggled my fingers, I nodded my head, I rolled over twice, I played my drum . . . Children can think of countless things to do. Each sets the pattern in turn, which is then followed by the others.*

1. As I was go-ing up Lon-don Hill, Lon-don Hill, Lon-don Hill, As I was go ing up Lon don Hill, On a cold, frost-y morn-ing.
2. I shook my head — *(children shake heads)* *(Sing)* I shook my head — *(children shake heads)* *(Sing)* On a cold, frost-y morn-ing.

44

# Little Marionettes

FRENCH NURSERY SONG

*Dangling fingers are the marionettes which dance gaily until "clap, clap, clap," is reached. For "three times round," one hand revolves around the other. This is an old French favorite.*

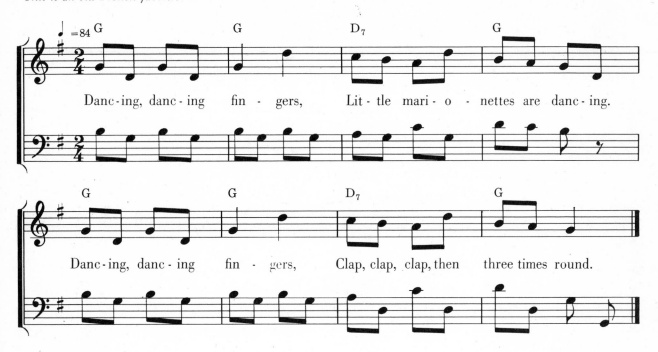

Danc-ing, danc-ing fin - gers, Lit-tle mari-o-nettes are danc-ing.

Danc-ing, danc-ing fin - gers, Clap, clap, clap, then three times round.

# My Mother Sent Me

ENGLISH SINGING GAME

*The messenger stands in the middle of the circle. At "to do with one as I do," he moves his first finger, making a pattern which the others follow as they sing the last two measures of the song. Children take turns at being messenger.*

My moth-er sent me un-to you. What to do? What to do? My moth-er sent me

un-to you, { 1. To do with "one" as I do. To do with "one" as I do.
2. To do with "two" as I do. To do with "two" as I do. [Etc.]

45

## The Ringmaster

WORDS AND MUSIC BY GRACE R. BURLIN.

*With a small length of rope for a whip, any small boy is proud to be ringmaster, while the children circle around. Dick said he'd be the horse, if they'd just imagine he had a lady on his back.*

The ring-mas-ter's whip goes a - snap! Crack! As a spot-ted white horse gal-lops round the track, With a beau-ti-ful la-dy up - on his back. Snap! Snap! Crack!

## The Lonesome Dove

AS SUNG IN KENTUCKY

*Miss T. taught this song with eager curiosity. Would the children jump up and "fly," when they found it was about a bird, or were they ready to sense the mood of a song? They were. Sara folded her arms about her head, saying, "This dove is sitting in a tree."*

1. Oh, don't you see that lone-some dove, That flies from vine to vine. It's
2. Just like I mourn for mine, my love; Be - lieve me what I say; You

mourn - ing for its own true love, Just like I mourn for mine.
are the dar - ling of my heart, Un - til my dy - ing day.

46

*Jack thought this horse didn't run fast because it was out of breath from "tearing around." The song sprouted many verses: "Nice big piano, but nobody's playing it" . . . "Good old chair, but nobody's sitting in it."*

# Old Gray Horse

FOLK SONG FROM ALABAMA

2.  Nice big horse,
    But there's nobody riding him,
    Nobody riding him,
    Nobody riding him.
    Nice big horse,
    But there's nobody riding him,
    'Way down in Alabam'.

3.  Great big fields about,
    Growing up in sassafras.
    'Way down in Alabam'.

4.  Great big white house,
    Nobody's living in it.
    'Way down in Alabam'.

47

# The Hippopotamus

WORDS AND MUSIC BY MARY BLATT KOCH

*Since there was no zoo in her town, Miss T. hunted for a big colored picture of a hippopotamus to show to the children. All of them—even Sara, the aesthete—thought the animal was beautiful.*

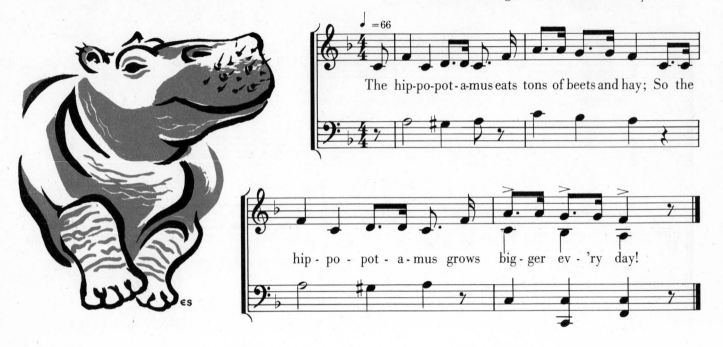

The hip-po-pot-a-mus eats tons of beets and hay; So the hip-po-pot-a-mus grows big-ger ev-'ry day!

# The Tiger

WORDS AND MUSIC BY GRACE R. BURLIN

*Because children are deeply interested in animals, they love to impersonate them. They seem to turn completely into tigers, as they stalk about the room and roar, delightedly, with rage.*

The ti-ger walks a-round and 'round _____ His paws are soft they make no sound _____ But when he roars the build-ing shakes, _____ So aw-ful is the noise he makes!

48

# Animal Sketches

BY WILLIAM GRANT STILL

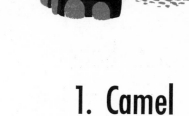

*Our little people have many delightful experiences being camels, bears, horses, lambs, and elephants, as this music is played. The movements of each are discussed. Elephants have such big feet they'd move heavily, wouldn't they? Bears are clumsy; lambs have long legs and frisk merrily about. Miss T. likes to use this music for discriminating listening. Her children are asked, "Would you rather be an elephant or a lamb?" Each child makes a choice, and lambs and elephants decide where each will live. When the elephants are all in one corner and the lambs in another, Miss T. begins playing. The children must listen to discover which will come first, "lamb music" or "elephant music." If it's "lamb music," out come the lambs into the middle of the room, where they perform until—suddenly—Miss T. switches to "elephant music," when the lambs run for the barn as the "elephants" come out of the jungle. The number of animals may be increased to three, then four, and finally five, as the children develop assurance in listening.*

## 1. Camel

*Swaying Movements*

## 2. Bear

*Ursine Clumsiness*

Moderately slow ( ♩ = 72 )

*mf*

# 3. Horse

# 4. Lamb

*Gamboling Movements*

Playfully ( ♩=112 )

*mp*

*mf*    *mp*

52

# 5. Elephant

**Ponderously** ( ♩ =72)

*f*

*simile*

*retard gradually* - - - - - - - - - - - - - - - - - - - - -

# Ponies

WORDS AND MUSIC BY GLADYS TIPTON

*This little song has a dramatic reason for slackening the tempo, so that children who impersonate the tired, tired pony become conscious of the fact they are moving more slowly at the end.*

See the po - ny, gal-lop-ing, gal-lop-ing, gal-lop-ing fast a - way;____

See the po - ny, gal-lop-ing, gal-lop-ing, gal-lop-ing back a - gain.____

See the po - ny walk-ing home, Slow, slow, slow____ Tired, tired, po - ny.

Although physical activity seems to be the outstanding characteristic of the pre-schooler, mental and emotional activity are also great. His free play often becomes dramatic reproduction of his real life experiences. This is his way of thinking them through. Thus our most effective dramatic plays will be based on plays suggested by the children or by their activities.

Children, everywhere, love to watch trains go by. Their attention may be called to the driving rods which roll the wheels. Back at school, they form in procession to make a train; their arms become driving rods which move the train uphill and down and through a tunnel (of chairs), with a dramatic slowing for stops as the "conductor" calls the name of nearby towns.

Children who live in the far West are familiar with the movements of tumble-weeds, and would enjoy a play based on their pranks as they roll in the wind. Where seagulls may be observed, a play may be invented in which feeding gulls are startled by children picking up shells on the beach. Midwestern children may be crows, with a scarecrow to startle them away.

Most children have experienced high winds, have braced their bodies against them and watched tree branches whipping back and forth. If so,

54

they would enjoy reliving this experience. Children in sections of the South visited by hurricanes might be palm trees, whipping about with vigorous axial movements as the center of the storm passes through.

The following rhythm drama was built on the responses of a five-year-old group to the question, "What different kinds of river things can you think of?" The teacher is the narrator; she weaves the children's ideas into a musical pattern, setting the stage and the mood by the dynamic changes in her voice, as well as by the instrumental accompaniment. (The accompaniment indicated is only suggestive; but serves to illustrate how simply it can be done. The clarity of the rhythm is the important element.)

The children have chosen their roles and are listening for their cues. The teacher watches the children as she plays and adjusts her tempo to their capacities and ideas.

"*It is early morning.* (Steady, slow repetition of quiet chords or thirds in upper register of piano.) *No one is up yet . . . The boats are tied up to the dock . . . The little waves rock them gently.* (Rocking rhythm on piano or on two drums of different timbre.) *The bell buoy rocks gently and calls, softly, 'Ding-Dong.' . . . The tall, tall lighthouse and the low, low rocks are still.* (Repeated chords, first high, then low.)

"*But deep in the water the fish are swimming smoothly, up and down.* (In a quickened, but smooth tempo, start low and go up and down scale.) *. . . And high in the sky the seagulls take their morning exercise. They stretch their wings . . . out over the water they glide . . . and back, back down to rest on the gentle waves.* (Same as fish music; start in middle register and go high up and back, keeping it *legato*.) *. . . Now the boats come out, first the fast speed boats . . .* (Quick chugging rhythm on piano or drum.) *. . . Then the slow, chugging boats.* (Same steady chords, but lower and twice as slow; or use drum of different timbre.) *Then both kinds together . . .* (Each hand represents one of these rhythms. Left hand plays a steady pedal bass for slow boats; right hand plays two beats to each left-hand beat, but moves stepwise up the scale.) *'Keep away from the rocks,' sings the bell buoy to the boats . . . The fish and the seagulls do not listen . . .* (Play their designated themes simultaneously.)

"*But look . . . a storm is coming up.* (Play a rumbling *crescendo*.) *The rain begins to fall . . .* (Staccato in piano's upper register or on triangle, played by a child; or both.) *The wind blows . . .* (Child may make sweeps on xylophone.) *The waves roll.* (Arpeggios.) *. . . The boats rock in the waves, b-i-g waves, b-i-g rocks.* (Big drum played by a child. The music has now combined the piano, triangle, xylophone, and drum, and has reached a climax in sound and action.) *. . . Slowly the wind dies down . . . The waves stop rolling. The boats stop rocking . . . The rain stops falling.* (Corresponding instrument, in turn, *diminuendos* to silence.) *The boats go back to their docks. First the fast ones . . . then the slow ones . . . They tie up . . . and go to sleep. So do the gulls . . . and the fish. Only the lighthouse shines . . . and calls 'Goodnight, Goodnight.'*"

The length of time devoted to such a drama, the determination of time allotted each character, and sequence of appearance must be flexible, dependent on the teacher's sensitivity to individual needs and also to the development of her musical theme. Thus a teacher might curtail or omit such an exciting climax as a storm, if her group tends to be easily overstimulated; or she might allow certain restless children longer and more frequent turns. Such a rhythm drama provides rich learning experiences.

Miss T. uses a play that gives the children a chance to differentiate between various emotions and their expression in movement and in music. "What do we do when we are very happy?" "We skip," says Sara. "Let's all skip happy," says Miss T., playing "happy music." Sometimes she quickly changes to sad music, to see if the children notice the difference. Almost all of them do. "How do we move to sad music?" Usually the children decide walking is best. "How do we move when we are very angry?" "Angry music" usually helps the children decide stamping is a good way to show they are angry; they love to move to it, with fists clenched and arms doubled up. Then when her children have had experience matching mood to music, Miss T. has the children group themselves into mad, sad, and happy groups, each in a different corner of the room. She plays music, in a different sequence each time. Each group moves to appropriate music.

# On the River

A RHYTHM DRAMA BY
MIRIAM BRODIE STECHER

# Variations on a Walk

CONTINUITY BY EDNA W. DOLL
MUSIC BY MARY JARMAN NELSON

### AREA OF ACTUAL EXPERIENCES

*1. Ordinary walk.* Children begin walking around the room. They LISTEN to their footsteps and establish a uniform rhythm. Leadership may develop in the group. Teacher picks up rhythm with tom-tom or this music:

*2. Walk with a definite objective.* "We're walking to school . . . you must meet your friend at the corner . . . he is waiting for you." *Or,* "Mother needs some bread, you are walking to the store."

*3. Fast walk (increasing tempo).* "We're going to catch a bus. Hurry, we're late." *Or,* "Your father is coming home. You're going out to meet him." Use wood block or Music B:

*4. Slow walk.* "We've been at the zoo all afternoon . . . You are very tired . . . it's four blocks to your home." Sand blocks or Music C:

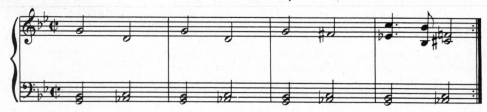

### AREA OF PRETENDING

The aim is to develop a slow walk with large, heavy steps and, in contrast, a small walk with short, light steps; also, to help children to learn to walk in a circle. Children have the ability to change quickly from one thing to another without lengthy explanation. The results are achieved by suggesting that the children pretend to be various characters or animals.

*1. Lumbering walk.* Children are giants or elephants. Gong or Music D:

56

2. *Fanciful walk.* Children are fairies. Light taps on tambourine or Music E:

3. *Shuffling walk.* Children make a train. Use sand blocks or Music F:

4. *Stately processional.* "Have you seen a wedding? Perhaps someone you know got married. Pretend you are in the wedding party . . . and you are walking down the aisle." ( Use Bridal Chorus from "Lohengrin." )

5. *Shuffling walk.* "The people went on the train for their wedding trip. In the open country the train sped along . . . it slowed for the crossings . . . and coming into the station . . . and finally stopped." Use Music H:

6. *Walking in a circle.* "The people went to a zoo. They walked around *this* cage, looking at the animals. Then they went to the *next* cage and walked around it. Use Music A. (Children form circle for cage; then successively imitate bears, rabbits, penguins, inside cage.)

7. *Skimming walk (light shuffling).* "Then they went home in an airplane."

> *Other suggestions:* Instead of using even weight on both feet, try limping. Discover the element of surprise in the "kick-walk." (Individuals will vary in their patterns. Some will kick every other step, some may "One, two, *kick*" or "One, two, three, *kick*.") There may also be directional variations. Children may walk forward, backward, sideways or across the diagonal, changing direction at the sound of a gong. Children may make up patterns, "Make up your own pattern, in your little patch; four steps each way."

57

## Mr. Fox

ENGLISH SINGING GAME

*As the year goes by and our children grow used to playing with other children, they become ready for stories that have more than one character. Miss T. begins simply, by transforming a game of tag into a fox hunt.*

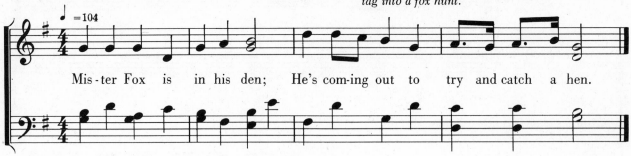

Mis-ter Fox is in his den; He's com-ing out to try and catch a hen.

## The Old Gray Goose

AMERICAN FOLK SONG

*Boys will be boys—and girls, girls. Already our little people are conscious of all this. Gaily they play at being goose and gander—birds which country children find in their yards and city children hunt for in the zoo.*

Look a-right here, And look a-right there, Look way o-ver yon-der,

Don't you see the old gray goose a-smil-in' at the gan-der? A-

smil-in', A-smil-in', A-smil-in' at the gan-der?

58

*This song was reserved for a day when most of the children were absorbed in cutting out pictures and only a few came for rhythms. It's so hard to wait for a turn at the role of stretching, sleepy cat.*

# The Little Cat

WORDS FROM THE FRENCH
MUSIC BY LAURE COLLIN

1. The pus-sy cat a-wak-ens, Perks up her ears to lis-ten, Then
2. Her face she slow-ly wash-es, With her two paws she rubs it. "Oh,

slow-ly looks a-bout her. "Good day, my pus-sy cat,— good day!"
come to one who loves you; Please come, my pus-sy cat,— come play!"

*As the children sing, the cat awakens in the center of the circle. Each of the children tries to bid "Good day" to the cat in a specially endearing way, so that he will be chosen as "the one who loves you." The one chosen by the cat as master or mistress has the next turn.*

59

# Song and Dance of the Pigs

WORDS FROM AN OLD FRENCH NURSERY RHYME
MUSIC BY LILLIAN BALDWIN

*Here is a longer story for a larger group, with several main characters. No child needs to sit on the sidelines, as all enjoy being one of the pigs, who run away, return, and dance together, as the dance is played after the song is sung.*

When I was a lit-tle fel-low, Youp, la, la, lol-ly lay!

I was guard-ing pigs all day, Youp, la, lol-ly, la lay!

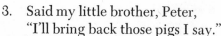

2. As I took them through the meadow,
   Youp, la, la, lolly lay!
   Ho, my pigs all ran away.
   Youp, la, lolly, la lay!

3. Said my little brother, Peter,
   "I'll bring back those pigs I say."

4. Peter took his merry bagpipes,
   And a jolly tune did play.

5. When they heard the bagpipes playing,
   Loudly squealing, back came they.

6. By their hoofs they took each other,
   And began to step and sway.

7. Then they made each other curtsies,
   And my pigs all danced away!

60

# The Dance

61

# Jack in the Box

WORDS AND MUSIC BY ELOISE LISLE JOHNSON

*The dramatic demands of this song are purposely simple, so that the children may concentrate on a new problem—action at a precise place in the music—as indicated by the words.*

I'm a jack-in-the-box, you see! Up I pop! Down I drop!

Oh, what fun I do have, you see! Pop-ping up and down!___

# Hop Up, My Ladies

FOLK SONG FROM VIRGINIA

*Cooperative planning is called for, if three children are to hop up at the right place in this song. Miss T. lets her children decide which three are to have the first turn and which will follow.*

Hop up, my la-dies, three in a row, Hop up, my la-dies, three in a row,

Hop up, my la-dies, three in a row, Don't mind the wea-ther, so the wind don't blow.

62

# John the Rabbit

AMERICAN FOLK GAME-SONG
ARRANGED BY JOHN W. WORK

*John, himself, illustrates for your children the many things they'll enjoy doing, on different days, as the "Oh, yes," is sung. Miss T.'s children make rabbit ears with hands over head. These waggle as all sing "Oh, yes," and—then—waggle as all keep silent on each "Oh, yes." The effect is fine.*

Oh, yes!

♩=84 e min.

Old John the rab-bit, Oh, yes! Old John the rab-bit, Oh, yes!

Got a might-y bad hab-it, Oh, yes! Of go-ing to my gar-den,

Oh, yes! And eat-ing up my peas, Oh, yes! And cut-ting down my cab-bage,

Oh, yes! He ate to-ma-toes, Oh, yes! And sweet po-ta-toes,

Oh, yes! And if I live, Oh, yes! To see next fall,

Oh, yes! I won't plant, Oh, yes! A gar-den at all!

I    IV

# Bow, Belinda

AMERICAN SINGING GAME

*Our little people feel big when they can dance real "dances," like older sisters and brothers. In this one, boys and girls are in facing lines. In the first verse, girls bow to partner in opposite line, with whom they swing around, during verses 2-4.*

♩ =92

1. Bow,— bow, bow Be-lin-da; Bow,— bow, bow Be-lin-da;
2. Right hand round, Oh, Be-lin-da; Right hand round, Oh, Be-lin-da;

Bow,— bow, bow Be-lin-da; You're the one my dar-ling.
Right hand round, Oh, Be-lin-da; You're the one my dar-ling.

3. *Left hand round, Oh, Belinda;*          4. *Both hands round, Oh, Belinda;*

# The Old Brass Wagon

SINGING GAME—INDIANA VERSION

*Children who have developed the ability to respond physically to a set signal are ready for a simple dance with words telling them what to do. In this game, they move around the circle, into the center and out, with hands clasped throughout.*

♩ =104

1. Cir-cle to the left, the Old Brass Wag-on; Cir-cle to the left, the Old Brass Wag-on;
2. Cir-cle to the right, the Old Brass Wag-on; Cir-cle to the right, the Old Brass Wag-on;
3. Ev-ery-bod-y in, the Old Brass Wag-on; Ev-ery-bod-y in, the Old Brass Wag-on;
4. Ev-ery-bod-y out, the Old Brass Wag-on; Ev-ery-bod-y out, the Old Brass Wag-on;

Cir-cle to the left, the Old Brass Wag-on; You're the one, my dar-ling.
Cir-cle to the right, the Old Brass Wag-on; You're the one, my dar-ling.
Ev-ery-bod-y in, the Old Brass Wag-on; You're the one, my dar-ling.
Ev-ery-bod-y out, the Old Brass Wag-on; You're the one, my dar-ling.

64

*Through dances, children come to realize that music is made of different parts. Miss T. never uses technical names; but her children know there are two parts to this dance, as they do two entirely different things.*

# Willowbee

PLAY SONG FROM THE DEEP SOUTH

(A) Refrain ♩ = 88

This way you wil-low-bee, Oh, wil-low-bee, Oh, wil-low-bee,___ This way you

wil-low-bee ___ All night ___ long. Oh,

(B) Verse

1. Danc-in' down the al-ley,
2. Skip-pin' down the al-ley,
3. Fly-in' down the al-ley,
4. Skat-in' down the al-ley,

al-ley, al-ley, Danc-in' down the al-ley, all night long.
al-ley, al-ley, Skip-pin' down the al-ley, all night long. Oh,___
al-ley, al-ley, Fly-in' down the al-ley, all night long.
al-ley, al-ley, Skat-in' down the al-ley, all night long.

*Big folks in the deep south "willowbee" by rocking back and forth on heel and toe. Our little people like to invent a pattern of their own—something they find amusing—as they sing from A. to B. At B. two lines of children form to make an "alley." Miss T. nods to a couple. The children dance down the alley any way they choose—swimming, jumping, rolling, sliding; they return as B. repeats. Part A. is then resung. Then Miss T. chooses another couple. "Tony and Barbara, how are you going down the alley?" B. is sung for them, with words appropriate to the movement they choose. Miss T. finds that returning to A. between each trip down the alley gives the children the security of a return to the familiar and serves to alleviate the monotony of waiting in line.*

# Folk Dance from "Hansel and Gretel"

ENGELBERT HUMPERDINCK

Broth-er come and dance with me, Both my hands I of-fer thee; Left foot first,

right foot then, Turn a-round and back a-gain. I would dance but don't know how,

When to clap or when to bow; Show me what I ought to do, So that I may

dance like you. With your foot you tap, tap, tap! With your hands you

clap, clap, clap! Left foot first, right foot then, Turn a-round and back a-gain.

CHAPTER FOUR

Courtesy Peripole Products, Inc.

## DISCOVERING SOUND

Little children can find music in water coolers, zippers, blocks, and drinking glasses. Miss T. makes sure they hear beautiful sounds, too. In an out-of-the-way corner are many instruments. Here, where they can really listen, her children explore the world of sound. Nail kegs and barrels are used for drums, but drum heads are of really fine quality. She can't afford Balinese instruments;[5] but metal objects, contributed by parents, give a fine ring. A wide variety of sound-making materials is provided, as well as the usual instruments.[6]

Her children are free to use the instruments, to take them about the room, or onto the playground, where sounds do not disturb the rest of the school. Naturally the instruments that give so much joy are carefully treasured; there is a ceremony of putting them to sleep beneath blankets before the children go home. Sometimes, when Miss T.'s ears get too tired, they take a nap, too.

At first, children go from one instrument to another, exploring the sound. Before long, some child discovers that a bell enhances the game of fireman. "All the firemen are asleep," says Tony, "I'll ring the bell and they'll wake and run to the fire." Sand blocks for a choo-choo sound, gongs and marimba for water sounds, blocks for hammering like a shoemaker, or a woodpecker on a tree, the click of castenets when children impersonate ducks . . . all these sounds enliven dramatic play, bring it closer to real-life situations.

# PLAYING INSTRUMENTS

Hilary stamps the snow from his boots. ( ♩ ♩ ♩ ) At intervals all morning he returns to this heavy stamping pattern. Later he transfers it to the biggest drum he can find. Another child may beat on a block and say, "This is the way the old witch ran away" or "This is the horse galloping." Yes, "imaginative use of instrumental rhythms comes first by way of movement."[3]

Interestingly enough, the instrument used when the child is primarily concerned with rhythm is relatively unimportant to him. The teacher can find ways to help children combine interest in timbre and rhythm. Miss T.'s children sing a rain song, one rainy day, imitating the patter of rain with their fingers, on the floor. When the rhythm of the rain has become thoroughly conscious, Miss T. says, "John, would you like to choose an instrument that sounds like rain pattering down? We'll close our eyes and listen, and see if we can guess which one you choose." While the children sing and patter with their fingers, John plays the xylophone.

67

# Burlesque Band

ENGLISH MUSICAL GAME

*To keep interest keen, Miss T. often adds new instruments to her collection and puts away old ones. After her children have explored the sounds of the new instruments, new stanzas are added.*

1. Oh,___ we can play on the tam-bour-ine, and this is the mu-sic to it;
2. Oh,___ we can play on the rhy-thm sticks, and this is the mu-sic to it;

Clinkle-inkle-ink, goes the tam-bour-ine, and this is the way we do it.
Tick, tick, tick, goes the rhy-thm stick, and this is the way we do it.

# Ki-yi-yi-yi

WORDS AND MUSIC BY MARY BLATT KOCH

*Miss T.'s little Indians dance around a council fire comprised of children impersonating leaping flames. By using different drums, this song can become a war or rain dance, or some other kind.*

Ki - yi - yi - yi, Ki - yi - yi - yi, In - dian beats his drum Ki - yi - yi - yi,

(Indian war whoop)

Ki - yi - yi - yi, beats his big red drum, Wah!___

68

8va

Almost every child knows this old favorite when he comes to school. When bells are discovered in the instrument corner, likely some child will shake them happily and begin to sing this song. Other children will come running, wanting to join in the fun. At this moment, the following activity might be found helpful, since it uses all the children and all the bells available. It builds from free, unpatterned movement into a real, little performance suitable for a Thanksgiving or Christmas program. (For the former, the song "Over the River and Through the Woods" might be more appropriate.) All sorts of additions and creative variants are possible. Miss T.'s Tony insisted, last Christmas, that Rudolph, the Red-nosed Reindeer, be enlisted to lead the horses. Of course Santa occupied the sleigh. It is possible to develop the entire activity at one time. It may also be spaced over several days.

1. All the children are trotting horses. The weather is cold and they feel frisky. They trot with high, light steps.

2. The snow begins falling. All the children become snowflakes, skimming lightly about the room. Fluttering fingers imitate flakes blown by the wind.

3. Half the children are horses, who must keep to the road (a general line about the room). The other half are snowflakes blowing about in many directions among the horses.

4. Finally the children build a horse-drawn sleigh. (See marginal diagram.) Two children ride inside the sleigh to the end of the room, where the horses circle and bring the sleigh and occupants back to the "barn."

# Jingle Bells

ACTIVITY BY EDNA DOLL

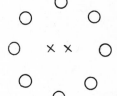

*Little people love to "make a parade," even before they can march or beat "in time." Oatmeal boxes may be made into portable drums, so that every child has a drum for this song.*

# Drum Song

WORDS AND MUSIC BY LILLIAN BALDWIN

A - rub-a-dub dub, A - rub-a-dub dub, We're march-ing down the street;___ For when the drum is pass - ing by, It runs a-way with our feet.___

# Boutique Fantasque

FRENCH NURSERY SONG

After many experiences, children are asked to listen to simple music. "What instruments does this music make us want to play?" Surely someone will suggest a tambourine for these triplets.

70

CONTINUITY BY EDNA DOLL

*Miss T. picks up a heavy step with the drum. "Can someone move another way?" Skips suggest tambourines, hops suggests woodblocks or castanets. After much practice in matching sound and movement, the children are ready for this story.*

"One day, in the forest, there is a huge giant, walking back and forth, back and forth, looking very cross.

*(A selected child dramatizes the giant) Tom-tom accompanies his walking rhythm*

"He stops and stretches his long arms. He lies down on the grass and falls sound asleep.

"There are children hiding behind a hedge and they peek out at him, this way and that way. . . .

*(Children sway from side to side in unison) Sand block*

"One brave child parts the hedge and steps through. All the other children are amazed at his courage.

*(A child acts brave)*

"This brave fellow walks all around the giant. Then he beckons to the other children and says: 'Come on.'

*Tom-tom*

"So the children step through the hedge cautiously, and tiptoe over to look at the giant. They bend over to see him more closely.

*(Trunks bend forward, then up, forward and up)*

"The giant sleeps on and on. One boy is a show-off. He says, 'I'm going to jump over the giant's legs' . . . and he DOES!

*(Leap) Cymbals*

"He turns around and says to the other children, 'I dare you to do it too.' One by one, they all jump over his legs. The last child trips and falls.

*(Leaping successively in rhythm) Light cymbal taps Loud cymbal crash*

"This wakes the giant and he sits up quickly. The children are frightened and run toward the hedge.

*Tambourine shakes*

"The giant calls, 'Children, come here!' They turn around, and are surprised that he is a kind and friendly giant.

"So they make a ring around him and do a lively dance.

*(Children skip lightly in one direction, accompanied by taps on tambourine. At a loud knock on the instrument, they reverse directions.)*

"The giant smiles because he is happy.

"He tells the children why he was walking up and down and looking so cross. Do you know why? He was lonesome and wanted someone to play with him.

"So every day the children came back to the forest for a game with the lonesome giant."

# The Orchestra

WORDS AND MUSIC BY MARY JARMAN NELSON

*Children eventually group themselves together to play instruments, with results that sound disorganized only to adults; for the players stop and correct one another. Miss T. knows, then, that they are ready for music with set signals.*

Click, click, click goes each lit-tle stick, Bum, bum, bum goes the drum;

*Words are to be chanted, not sung. Chant rhythm which differs from piano part is notated above the words.*

Ting, ting, ting-a-ling-a-ling, Lis-ten to the tri-an-gle sing.

Shake, shake the tam-bour-ine, sounds like gyp-sies danc-ing. Tap-a-tap-a,

tap-a-tap-a, tap, tap, tap, sounds like pon-ies pranc-ing!

Knock, knock, knock on the lit-tle wood block, Who is the next in line?

72

Ah, I see Mis-ter Cym-bal there, Get read-y, get SET, SHINE! *rit.*

Soft and slow the mus - ic, Down, down, down._____

L. L. L.

Soft and slow the mus - ic, Up,* up,* up.*

*Teacher:* Now would you like to have a tune that everyone can play? *Children:* Yes.

*a tempo*

*Teacher:*

Five young peo - ple in a row, March-ing off to Buf-fa-lo;

They will get there ver - y soon.

*Teacher:* When will they get there?

*Very fast*

*Children:*

They'll be there by this af - ter-noon!

# Playing the Piano

BY MARY JARMAN NELSON

*In their experimentation with sound, through instruments, children discover melody-making, too. Likely as not, it is on that most common of all instruments—the kindergarten piano.*

The piano can be an endless source of enjoyment to small children and a great aid in their musical development, *if* they are allowed to play it.

The first fascination is usually one of manipulation. The keys can be pushed down to make sound. And they come back up!

*Mary Ann was charmed by her slow two-finger trill on adjacent keys. Miss T. allowed her to go to the piano at frequent intervals throughout one day, because the sound did not bother the other children. When wraps were on, and everyone was waiting for parents, the children asked for a song. Miss T. suggested that Mary Ann play "way up here," between the stanzas of "Little Redbird" (page 9), as everyone sang. She was, in turn, the redbird, bluebird, and blackbird.*

*Hilary was challenged by the piano keyboard, taking it as something to be accomplished in its entirety. Each day, when his turn came to play, he would "walk" slowly from the bottom to the top, playing every white key. One rainy day, when they could not go outdoors, Miss T. suggested that they pretend "Jungle Gym" (page 40), climbing from a crouched position on the floor to high stretches on tiptoe, while Hilary furnished the music.*

Other children are drawn to the instrument by the *feel* as well as the *sound*, by the sensation of the smooth cool keys against arms and palms.

*Tom, who had never touched a piano before coming to school, played first with his elbows, then with both forearms, encompassing two octaves. The group agreed that some of his music was "too hard." However, it furnished a good explosive ending for the BOOM, when they played "Sally Go Round the Moon" (page 33).*

Flat little palms and loose, relaxed fists can play "tone clusters." These are helpful in underlining the rhythmic vitality of familiar music and as percussive effects in rhythmic play and dramatization.

*The drum needed repairing. So, to furnish drum music for a parade, Aaron played the three black keys in the low register, simultaneously, with both hands.*

*After singing "Let's Take a Little Trip" (page 23), the children wanted to play train. Tony improvised some fine train music, with palms flat on the keys. He started slowly, then picked up speed as the train sped across the meadows. He added a high whistle at the crossing, then made a beautiful* ritardando *as he came to a stop at the station.*

The character of the piano's various registers can add color to daily sound experiences, and help children in developing discrimination.

*The group was playing animals. Three children were chosen to furnish the piano music. Barbara's kangaroo leaped about over the keyboard.*

74

*Peter's hippopotamus was slow and clumsy; it was made of heavy chords in the bass. Peter put down the pedal and held the tones for a long, long time. The group called, "Go on." He calmly replied, "The hippo is resting. He's tired."*

*Jean's chattering monkeys were high in the trees (treble and rapid staccato); but one of them took a swing with his tail to another tree. (A quick roll of Jean's arm to another octave.)*

Piano improvisation, with a little guidance by the teacher, can heighten the dramatic effect of such familiar songs as "Busy Trucks" (page 24), "Drum Song" (page 69), "Our Windshield Wiper" (page 22).

*The highlight of Halloween music came just after a singing of "The Witch Rides" (page 97). Jane, standing beside the piano, picked up her pinafore and made a sweeping glissando to the top of the keyboard.*

Spontaneous piano playing is not always noisy and dramatic. Sometimes it is poetic and restful.

*Sara came in early from play. Miss T. found her seated at the piano with a book (upside down) on the music rack. She was playing soft music with alternating hands rising high into the air, and singing a sleepy tune of her own. Miss T. said nothing. Later, when rest time came, Sara was asked if she would like to put the children to sleep with some quiet music. As she played, softly, she whispered, "I'm the moon, playing my baby stars to sleep."*

As young children experiment, discover, and create, they show a growing desire to fit their piano music into tonal and rhythmic patterns which conform to grown-up music ways. They quickly learn that some of the keys look alike (the black ones are the easiest to identify), and feel a great joy of accomplishment when playing a "ground bass" on the same keys throughout a familiar song. Harmonic changes (from I to IV or V7) are not important to very small children. One or more children can stand on the teacher's left, throughout "Knock Along, Brother Rabbit" (page 29). While the teacher plays the tune, the children play these tones:

Other suggestions: "Old King Glory" (page 33) (Same as above)

"Marching Song of the Shepherds" (page 114)

"One Day One Foot Kept Moving" (page 42)

For songs of a lighter character, the children may stand at the right of the teacher:  "Chicken Licken" (page 84)

"Who's That Knocking At My Door?" (page 14)

"The Marines' Hymn" is a great favorite both at school and at home (page 116). This is a good study in form and also in quick key location. The child plays a B flat with each hand, during the first sixteen measures. At the words "First to fight," where the harmony changes to A flat, he marches—like a Marine!—around the piano and returns to his two keys on the piano at the words, "We are proud . . ." (or, as he will say, "when the music sounds like the first.") He will be too extravagant with his marching during the first few trials; but will eventually "dash right into duty" at the right place.

Going a little further, the young pianists will want to be helped to play at a *certain time*, in the music. Their old friend "John the Rabbit" is a good starter. Teacher finds the key for five people who stand at the piano and play on "Oh, yes!" A next step is filling in the rest with repeated notes after "when she comes" in the first, second, and last phrases of "She'll Be Comin' Round The Mountain." These echo notes are harder; the children play first A flats, then B flats, then back to A flat.

The ingenious teacher can discover many fragmentary passages in the children's songs which are adaptable to a child's piano-playing. Especially good are the endings of songs, such as "Skip to my Lou, my darling" (page 34); or, in "Lavender's Blue" (page 17), the final ". . . you shall be queen."

The piano can add interest to many tales.

 *Shelby liked a chord his brother had shown him. So, as the group heard the story of "The Old Woman and the Pig," Shelby played a resolute "No," with the chord, as each character in the story refused the old woman's request. He also "invented" this chord for the cooperative cow in the story:*

*Sylvia's mother had taught her the song about the gingerbread man on the black keys. With great pride, Sylvia showed the children how it went. After that, the children were never satisfied with the story unless the piano could sing the part of the gingerbread man.*

Melodic recreation of known songs, at the piano, is vitally necessary to some children.

*After experimenting for a while, on the black keys, Barbara called, "Listen, I've found it! This sounds like 'Rudy, Rudy, Rannie.' Help me find the rest of it." This tune can be played entirely on the black keys, also "Two in the Middle" (page 30). Other tunes were found which fitted the black keys. The proudest day of Barbara's five and a half years was the Monday morning on which she announced she had played "Jesus Loves Me," in Sunday School.*

*The day that Mary Ann was five, Miss T. showed her how to play the "1, 2, 3, 4, 5" and the "blow them out" of "Birthday Song" (page 96). Her mother reported that she entertained the family party that night so persistently with this piano performance, that finally Uncle Morton made a tape recording of it for the family collection.*

With teacher's guidance, each group will work out its own regulations for piano-playing. Turn-taking is fair and usually accepted. Requests will often come for some particular child to play, because "Sara knows some tunes." This may give Sara or Paul a sense of security lacking during other activities.

## CHAPTER FIVE

## THE ROOTS OF MUSIC APPRECIATION

As Paul beat out the rhythm of a trotting horse on the floor, Miss T. silently handed him the tom-tom. The child hesitated but an instant, then transferred his rhythm to the instrument, showing obvious satisfaction with the new sound, as he did so. Another day, Jean was dragging a stick across the radiator. When Miss T. imitated the motion on the xylophone, Jean came running at once. "Which one sounds prettier, Jean?" Miss T. asked. Jean only smiled and reached for the mallet, whereupon Miss T. withdrew, feeling that her little lesson in music appreciation had been completely successful.

Music, Miss T.'s way, is always more fun than noise. Thus listening, discriminative listening, proceeds day by day. As the year goes by, the children listen more carefully, more appreciatively, as Miss T. sings to them, or as one of the group sings or plays a bit on the piano or on another instrument. Music is so much a part of life with Miss T.—a life full of respect for each child—that without thinking about it, the children develop respect for music, itself.

Of course, they are asked to listen when they pick up a child's rhythm on the drum, or when they move with music that is "sad, mad, or glad." They have to listen, too, in order to decide if it's lamb or elephant music. And then, in addition to the listening experiences that come naturally during the day, Miss T. provides other experiences with music that help little ears to develop.

*Courtesy Harris and Walton*

# LISTENING TO MUSIC

Mary Ann had played with the woodblock for days on end. One day she discovered that hitting it in the center made a sound different from that made by hitting on the outside. Eagerly, she ran to tell Miss T. Her excitement attracted a small group. "What does it sound like?" asked Miss T., striking both places, alternately.

"*Tick . . . tock*, like a clock," Robin volunteered.

"Shut your eyes, now," Miss T. said. "Is this sound a *tick* or a *tock*?"

After some practice, most of the children could tell whether it was *ticks* or *tocks* that they heard.

"Now half of you are *ticks* and half *tocks*. Raise your hands as Jean plays your sound." A fascinating game was evolved. Miss T. then played a high note on the piano for the *ticks* and a low one for the *tocks*. Soon the children were able to make piano responses, too. A clock song was finally sung. Of course there was an accompaniment on all the woodblocks. (All this took only sixteen minutes.)

# Listening Throughout the Day

WITH RECORD SUGGESTIONS FOR IMPLEMENTNG THE LISTENING PROGRAM

*Music for performance to young children is usually selected in conformity with adult ideas of simplicity and suitability. Supposed melodic unsophistication, rhythmic uncomplexity and lack of harmonic subtlety are what are sought. Combined with this there is often a pernicious desire to superimpose stories or pictures upon the music, and music actually or ostensibly based upon a literary "program" is felt to be particularly suited to the child's needs. From our observations we are able to offer the following logical criticisms of these practices: 1. The child's melodic concepts, and therefore his sense of melodic simplicity, are different from those of the conventional musical world and obviously cannot be judged or satisfied by adult standards. 2. The child has a very complex consciousness of rhythm and requires only that the rhythms he hears be dynamic and generated by impulses which he can feel. 3. To the child all harmony is complicated; there is for him no qualitative difference between tonic-dominant harmony and that which uses altered chords and chromatic progressions. 4. His primary interest is in* SOUNDS *as things in themselves, not in musical story telling which is a complicated process involving much symbology. The child should hear much music, interesting in tone color, short and rhythmically dynamic, played by many different kinds of instruments—solo and in small instrumental combinations. He should hear not only the instrumental and vocal music of our culture, and especially our folk music, but also that of the Balinese, Javanese, Siamese, Chinese and Japanese peoples, and the instrumental music and songs and chants of primitive races. And he should have opportunity and guidance so that he can relate the sounds he hears to their counterparts in his experiential and creative environment.*

MUSIC OF YOUNG CHILDREN; II. GENERAL OBSERVATIONS
PILLSBURY FOUNDATION FOR ADVANCEMENT OF MUSIC EDUCATION

## FOLKWAYS RECORDS

DRUMS OF HAITI—Features percussion: *Vodoun Dance; Ibo Dance; Salongo Juba; Congo Payette; Congo Larose Mascaron; Baboule; Bumba; Ganbos; Vaccines.*

INDONESIA—Music of Bali, Malaya, Java and Sumatra.

MIDDLE EAST–PALESTINE—Music from cross roads of Europe, Asia and Africa. Bokharian: *Love Song; Wedding Dance.* Hebrew: *Prayer; Songs.* Persian: *Recitation.* Yemen: *Ceremonial Songs.* Arabic: *Recitation from the Koran; Songs.*

FOLK MUSIC OF INDIA—Songs of West Bengal, Haryana, Tamil, Rajastan and South India.

FOLK MUSIC OF PERU—Music of the Mestizo, Quechua and Aymara Indians, featuring harp, charango, quena flutes, horns and drums.

MIDDLE EAST–BUKHARA, UZBEKISTAN, AZERBAIJAN and ARMENIA—Representing cultures of Transcaucasus and Central Asia. Dances and folk songs played on native instruments: tar, tambur, doira, nai and rebeb.

AMERICAN INDIANS OF THE S. W.—Music of various Indian tribes: San Ildefonso, Taos, Zuni, Hopi, Yuma, Western Apache, Havasupai, Navajo, Walapai, Papago, So. Athabascan, Pueblo, Plateau Yuma, Rancheria.

MUSIC OF SOUTH ARABIA—Bedouin tribes in western protectorate, Yemen in Aden, documentary meeting of tribes. *Sword Dance; War Song; Yemen Love Song* and *Wedding.*

MUSIC OF INDIA, VOL. 2—Traditional and classic instrumental and vocal *Ragas.* This music is heard in stylized dances and in motion pictures depicting Indian life in court and city.

. . . "And all that," said Miss T. to the PTA president, "boils down to the fact that I've got to have a record player and quantities of records. I can sing to the children. I can play a pipe for them, which they dearly love to hear, and strum American folk music on an autoharp. But I can't play orchestral instruments or furnish authentic Balinese, Javanese, or Japanese music on native instruments. So I'll cooperate in a strawberry festival or square dance, or any other way you choose to raise the money; but I've got to have a record player that's really good. Since it's sound that interests the children most, that sound should be of fine quality."

Instrumental sound—what a boundless world for adventure. Everywhere, from earliest times, men have plucked strings, fashioned pipes, and pounded on metal or wood. Recapturing these impulses . . . the dynamic rhythms that men transferred to their instruments . . . is like holding a finger on the pulsating heartbeat of history itself.

"But we have to remember that pre-schoolers aren't concerned with history, or geography, or musicology." Miss T. was talking to the parents' committee that came to help select records, when the money had been raised. "Let's just kick off our shoes and listen the way the children do. They want

78

music that is alive . . . that moves . . . that makes them want to move, too."

"I suppose this one is out," said Mr. F., fingering a cello recording.

"I don't see why," said Miss T., "we're not going overboard on the exotic, the outré. As I see it, the Pillsbury people aren't excluding the music of our Western world. They say children will eventually accept it naturally, as their cultural heritage; but will bring to it richer perception if they've also absorbed the music of other cultures, at an age when all sound seems natural to them.

"However," she continued after a pause, "why should we spend our precious money on cello records, when you can bring your cello to school? You can play all sorts of nice, short things that haven't even been recorded. That way our children can see and even touch a cello, as well as listen to it. I've always counted on our high school students to supply experiences with instruments, but no one is playing a cello this year."

"I'll come," Mr. F. said, putting down the cello recording.

"How about songs?" Mrs. M. asked.

"We'll have people come to sing, too. Seeing the face of a singer helps so much. However, I do want recordings of some of our songs and some of the elementally simple songs that are ideal for basic rhythms.* There are times when the children and I are just too busy moving about to sing. I'd like *Come Lassies and Lads* for skipping, for instance."

When the committee reviewed the list that evolved, they found it contained many examples of folk music. Forthrightness . . . vitality . . . these qualities they found close to people, themselves.

"But I had wanted just a few luxuries," sighed Miss T. "Say Debussy's *The Snow Is Dancing*, from The Children's Corner. I'd love to slip that one on the first day it snows real hard, and just see what happens, without saying a word."

"I can lend you that one for the occasion," a committee member said. "We'll just have to hope the weather man is to be trusted."

Since stress was to be laid on folk music, the contributions from every land were to be treasured. Tony's father brought his concertina and Jose's uncle sang Mexican folk songs to the strumming of his guitar. (As a result of the reception the children accorded these performances, the mother of one of these boys came to school to visit, for the first time.)

"Leave it to music," said Miss T., contentedly, that night; thus summing up to her own satisfaction at least all that poets and philosophers have written over the years about the strangely wonderful powers of music. Yes, Miss T. believes music can be trusted. As a result of the commotion raised along with the money, parents all over town got interested in buying suitable records for their children. Miss T. found a home in her room for many of the records of which they had grown tired. Frequently her children are allowed to choose from the pile any that they want to hear. "If it's vital enough to stir their imaginations, it will do them good. If it's not, it will find its way to the bottom of the pile."

Often she, herself, is entranced with a record she tries out at home. Before the first excitement has worn off, she brings it to school to share; playing it,

* As an illustration of this point, Hey-Ho, Anybody Home, an old English round, has been included among the thirty-one selections recorded for use with this book. All these records feature the sounds of various instruments; this one will be found useful both as a lullaby and for rocking movement.

SOUTHEAST ASIA—A highly cultivated style characteristic of the area. Recorded in Burma, Malaya, Thailand, Viet Nam, Laos, South China. Includes: *Folk Songs; Ode; Love Songs; Dances; Recitation.*

MUSIC OF THE WORLD'S PEOPLES—Including music of: United States, Greece, Eire, Japan, Nigeria, Madagascar, India, Russian Gypsy, Bali, Iceland, Spain, Tahiti, Arabia, Tibet, France.

*The above mentioned records are obtainable from: Folkways Record and Service Corporation, 117 West 46th Street, New York, N. Y.*

## INSTRUMENTS

*The Nutcracker Suite*—Tchaikovsky
 "Dance of the Reed Flutes"
 "Dance of the Sugar Plum Fairy"
*Suite No. 2, B minor*—Bach
 "Badinerie"
*L'Arlésienne Suite*—Bizet
 "Prelude, Minuetto, Carillon"
*Symphony No. 7, C major*—Schubert
 "Andante," 1st theme
*Licorice Stick*—YPR
*Mother Goose Suite*—Ravel
 "Beauty and the Beast"
*Rondo for Bassoon and Orchestra*—YPR
*Carmen Suite*—Bizet
 "Changing of the Guard"
*Brandenburg Concerto No. 2*—Bach
*A Midsummer Night's Dream*—Mendelssohn
 "Nocturne"
*The Hunter's Horn*—YPR
*Lohengrin*—Wagner
 "Prelude to Act III"
*Tubby the Tuba*—Kleinsinger
*Romanian Folk Dances*—Bartok
*Goyescas*—Granados
 "Intermezzo"
*Poissons d'or*—Debussy
*Said the Piano to the Harpsichord*—YPR
*Concerto for Toy and Orchestra*—YPR
*Toy Symphony*—Haydn—YPR
*The Runaway Sheep*—YPR
*Little Indian Drum*—YPR
*Oraré* (jungle rhythm)—Decca
*Little Brass Band*—Hendl—YPR
*L'Histoire d'un Soldat*—Stravinsky
*Les Noces*—Stravinsky
*The Carnival of the Animals*—Saint-Saëns

*Scenes of Childhood*—Schumann
*Introduction and Allegro*—Ravel
*Peter and the Wolf*—Prokofieff
*The Children's Corner*—Debussy
*Basic Record Library* for Elementary
    Schools—RCA Victor
*New Music Horizons*—Columbia
    Volume One – "The Merry-Go-
      Round"
    Album 1, Series 2–"At the Circus"


## LULLABIES

*Lullaby*—Mozart
*Cradle Song*—Schubert
*Sweet and Low*—Barnby
*Lullaby*—Brahms
*Little Sandman*—Brahms
*Hush My Babe*—Rousseau
*Berceuse* from *The Fire Bird*—Stravin-
    sky
*Träumerei*—Schumann
*Evening Prayer* from *Hänsel and*
    *Gretel*—Humperdinck
*Berceuse*—Chopin


TAMBOURINE
    *La Calinda*—Delius


TRUMPET CALL
    *March of the Little Lead Soldiers*—
    Pierné


WATER SOUNDS
    *Reflets dans l'eau*—Debussy
    *Poissons d'or*—Debussy

CHICKENS
    *Hens and Cocks* from *The Carnival*
    *of the Animals*—Saint-Saëns


LUNCH TIME
    *Goyescas*—Granados
    "Intermezzo"

SLEEPY TIME
    *Träumerei*—Schumann

perhaps, while the children are busy with clay or cut outs. Not everyone will listen carefully, although the children lower their voices out of courtesy, realizing that this is Miss T.'s turn to play something she wants to hear. Usually several children, sensing Miss T.'s own genuine pleasure in the music, come to share the excitement, only to find that this music is speaking to them, too.

Thus slow movements from symphonies, concertos, or chamber music literature are heard as background music during block or lunch time, or as the children put on wraps to go outdoors. Such records are introduced without comment and are repeated at frequent intervals throughout the year, until the melody becomes a favorite with the children.

Occasionally there is a specific job for music to do. Lullabies and other quiet music soothes the children as they lie down to rest or when emotions are running high. Tension or discord may slip in while some of the children are painting. Miss T. has found that music that flows easily and rhythmically relaxes little arms and hands, thus freeing the children so that they may use their own best ideas and energies.

There are many occasions when the children sit about and give their undivided attention to listening. Miss T. never compels a child to listen if he feels he has something more important to do. She does insist that those who care to listen be allowed to do so. Whenever possible, this listening grows out of the children's own activities. Some child's experimentation with the tambourine, for instance, may have attracted the attention of other members of the group. As the interest begins to wane, Miss T. suggests listening to a dance by Delius which makes colorful use of this instrument.

Or the children may have been making a game out of calling to each other from various corners of the room. Before this play gets out of hand, Miss T. plays a record featuring trumpet calls and asks the children to hear how the trumpet calls all the other instruments into action.

One day when the children were tiring of playing *Community Helpers*, page 19, Miss T. played *The Volga Boat Song*. "Let's see if we can discover with our bodies what kind of work the men are doing as they sing this song."

Another day the children had sung and pantomimed *Ponies*, page 54. "Let's make the sound of a trotting pony with our hands." "Now listen to these horses . . ." Quickly she played a short section of *The Ride of the Valkyries*. "Can we clap the way these horses move? Are they trotting? It's different, isn't it?" The children guess how the horses move. Finally, Miss T. explains that these are story-book flying horses that brought home dead soldiers from the battlefield.

The children like to play musical guessing games, too. "This music is like what sound we all have heard?" The sound of water, the cackling of hens— Miss T. can find many real-life sounds in her record cabinet.

To add to their listening experiences, Miss T. uses bits of fine music for signalling the different activities of the day. By changing these signals frequently, she finds the children build up quite a repertory before the year is over. "This is our new lunch music," she will say one morning. "Listen carefully so you will know when you hear it again, it's time to come to lunch."

"How can we recognize it?" Little by little, the children learn to discern whether music is sad or happy, loud or soft, fast or slow, and when tones are high or low. Just as the need for discernment is made a part of their daily living by Miss T., so the experiences that now make discernment possible have been woven into their everyday activities.

Many of the imitative vocal or instrumental sound effects which children voluntarily use to accompany their rhythmic-dramatic play are likely to be realistic tonal pictures of their physical movement of *up* and *down*, *high* and *low*, and the like. Thus soaring balloons call for soaring voices, while the alternating up and down movement of a see-saw suggests a similar alternating up and down pattern in the accompanying singing voice.

One day Miss T. decides to make this conscious. After singing *Little Redbird in a Tree*, page 9, she will say, "Where on a piano shall we make a bird sing?" Little fingers match sounds and concepts and search for a thin sound, which they eventually find in the upper register. For a while all thin sounds are "bird music." Then, perhaps since many birds are seen high in trees, the children begin to adapt the adult fashion of terming thin sounds "high," and thick sounds "low."

After singing *Toot, toot the whistle blows*, page 23, Miss T. plays low on her pipe, saying, "How's this for a train whistle?"

"No, no," says John, doubled up with laughter. "Train whistles sound way up high." And he holds up his arms and stands on tiptoe to show her. This gives Miss T. an idea.

"Let's play statue," she calls. "Now I'm going to play some skipping music that goes both high and low. When I stop, suddenly, you are going to pose like a statue. If the music *stops high*, you are going to be a tall, high statue. If the music *stops low*, all the statues stop close to the ground."

This was so much fun that Miss T. made up similar games to play with instruments. "What instrument has a thin sound?" Sara chose a triangle. "What instrument has a big, thick sound?" Peter suggested a drum.

"I am going to play thick sounds and thin sounds on the piano. When I play thin sounds, Sara will play her triangle. When I play thick sounds Peter will play his drum."

Sara and Peter soon were able to make the desired responses, helped by the suggestions of all the children. Others took turns. A tambourine was added to play middle tones. This became a favorite guessing game.

Hilary hadn't seemed much interested that first day. On the day following he took Miss T.'s hand and led her to the piano. "Listen," he said. "This is the papa bear (playing low), this is the mama bear (playing around middle C), and this is the baby bear (at the very top of the piano)."

"Let's make a parade," Barbara said one day.

"I've got the big drum; I can't walk around with it. I'll play and make you gallop, walk and run," Jose replied.

Discernment of fast and slow comes easier to children than the adjustment of their bodies to extreme tempos. When the children were about to break up the parade, Miss T. stepped in. "I'm going to play a record. Let's see what this music makes us do—a slow walk, or a gallop or run."

At another time a group played their instruments together. Tom set the pattern that day, commanding the others to follow. "When I point to the door, it's going to be fast. When I point to the window it's going to be slow." Since Tom's bossiness frequently irritated his fellows, Miss T. stood by

PLAY TIME
*Sonata* in F minor, Op. 5—Brahms
"Scherzo"

GOING HOME TIME
*Siegfried*—Wagner
"Siegfried" theme

## BASIC RHYTHMIC MOVEMENT

WALK
*Air de Ballet*—Jodassohn
*Amaryllis*—Ghys
*March*—Hollaender

RUN
*Etude Joyeuse*—Kopylow
*The Pipers*—Gounod
*Happy and Light*—Balfe
*Sparks*—Moskowski
*Tarantelle*—Mendelssohn

SKIP
*Barcarolle*—Rubinstein
*Gigue in A*—Corelli
*Sicilienne*—Gluck

GALLOP
*The Wild Horseman*—Schumann
*Little Hunters*—Kullak
*Campbells Are Coming* — Scotch Folk Song

SWING OR ROCK
*Scherzo in B flat*—Schubert
*Skaters*—Waldteufel
*To a Water Lily*—MacDowell

JUMP OR HOP
*Jumping*—Gurlitt
*Polly Put the Kettle On*—Folk Song

MARCH
*March* from *Nutcracker Suite*—Tchaikovsky
*Soldiers March*—Schumann
*March* from *The Love For Three Oranges*—Prokofieff
*Bridal Chorus* from *Lohengrin*—Wagner

waiting for the time when she might be needed. "I'm going to play a record. When the music goes fast, we'll all point to the door. When it goes slow, we'll all point to the window."

Soft and loud also comes easily, and with this a sensing of mood as well. "We play a cymbal when the music crashes. We'll play our sticks when it tiptoes lightly." This is a game for songs and records alike.

Short and long is harder. Miss T. begins with a song about a frog. She asks, after the children have jumped about, whether they know any other creatures that hop or jump. A number are suggested, each with a realistic rhythmic dramatization. Joey says, "Some of them hop little, and some of them hop big, like a jump." Thereupon, hopping birds, crickets, and hop toads are compared with kangaroos, frogs, and jack rabbits, both in word and deed. Miss T. then plays two recordings, illustrating these kinds of rhythmic movement, the children interpreting each one.

Finally, as familiar music is played, balls are rolled between pairs of children seated on the floor facing each other, with ample distance between. The ball starts rolling at the beginning of a phrase. "See if we can roll it so it stops just as we hear the music come to a pause." This takes practice, but eventually the children are able to gauge speed and the length of a phrase with remarkable accuracy.

Some years the children develop more feeling for phrasing than others. It depends on the group and Miss T. never wearies her children by forcing the issue. "There's plenty of time, they'll get it easily later on." Some groups need plays of this sort toward the end of the year, so that music keeps fresh and new—always one step ahead for adventure. With very quick groups that develop a sure feeling for phrase length, Miss T. plays records like a Schubert Waltz, asking for a change of pattern of step, or direction, as the music moves from one phrase to another. Some years she is able to work up to movement by sections. Playing a simple rondo, she asks the children to move the same way when the music repeats and do something different during the contrasting sections.

## CHAPTER SIX

Courtesy Peripole Products, Inc.

## PARTICIPATING IN THE STORY

Today's children are given experiences with literature that foster oral responses. There is a place for musical responses, too. Indeed, with our little people, sometimes these cannot be prevented. "I know a song about a duck," says Robin, as he sees a duck picture on the page from which Miss T. plans to read. Robin sings and others get up and start to waddle like ducks. Has Miss T.'s story time been completely disrupted? Does she ask Robin to sit down? Soon . . . but not right away. For she remembers that appreciation for literature depends on growth in identifying oneself with the characters of the story. What better preparation for hearing about a duck than actually impersonating one?

Another story may have reiterated lines, like "The Old Woman and the Pig." Some children will speak these lines with Miss T., at a third or fourth hearing. Others may sing them. Miss T. will hear the catchy sentence played on instruments, as the days go by. (Repetition and music are already associated in her children's minds.)

All this participation heightens the feeling of children for literature, which, itself, grows from rich sensory experiencing, as well as from powerful feeling and deep thinking. The tales Miss T. sings, rather than tells, are more richly experienced because the children can join the cast of characters, riding along on the tune and coming in on the words as they remember them. Often they use their instruments to add a note of realism.

# TALES WITH TUNES

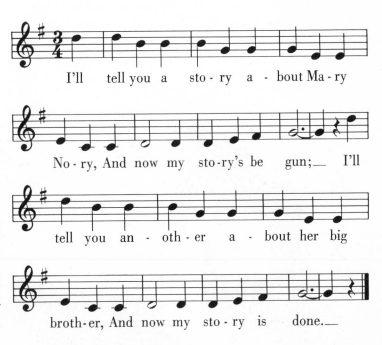

I'll tell you a sto-ry a-bout Ma-ry No-ry, And now my sto-ry's be gun;— I'll tell you an-oth-er a-bout her big broth-er, And now my sto-ry is done.—

# The Old Woman and the Little Pig

OLD TALE ARRANGED BY MARY JARMAN NELSON

Once upon a time this old woman went to market and bought a fat pig. On the way home, they came to a stile. The pig would not jump the stile. She scolded and begged but the pig wouldn't move.

The old woman saw a dog coming up the road, so she said, "Dog, please bite my pig and make him jump the stile." But the dog would not.

She saw a stick lying in the road, so she said, "Stick, please beat that dog, because:

"Dog won't bite pig, Pig won't jump stile; And I shan't get home 'til morn - ing."

But the stick would not.

So she began walking down the road and met some fire. She said, "Fire, please burn that stick." But the fire would not.

So she went on a little farther, and came to a stream of water. She said, "Water, please quench that fire, because:

"Fire won't burn stick, Stick won't beat dog;
Dog won't bite pig, Pig won't jump stile; And I shan't get home 'til morn-ing."

But the water would not.

About that time an ox came walking along. So she said, "Ox, *please* drink that water." But the ox would not. He just grinned at her.

So the old woman went along down the road until she came to a butcher shop. The butcher said, "Good morning, old woman, what can I do for you?"

So she said, "Butcher, butcher, *please* kill that ox, because:

"Ox  won't drink water,  Water won't quench fire;
Fire won't burn stick,  Stick won't beat  dog;
Dog won't bite  pig,  Pig  won't jump stile;  And  I shan't get home 'til  morn-ing."

But the butcher would not.

So she went a little farther and met a rope. She said, "Rope, *please* choke that butcher." But the rope would not.

Just then a rat ran across the road, and the old woman said, "Rat, *please* gnaw that rope, because:

"Rope won't choke butcher,  Butcher won't kill    ox;
Ox    won't drink water,  Water won't quench fire;
Fire   won't burn stick,  Stick won't beat    dog;
Dog won't bite  pig,  Pig  won't jump stile;  And  I shan't get home 'til  morn-ing."

But the rat would not.

As she walked on down the road, she met a cat. She said, "Cat, *please* eat that rat."

The cat licked her paws and thought a while. Then she said, "Old woman, if you'll go get me a saucer of milk from that cow over in the meadow, I'll kill the rat."

"Very well," said the old woman. So she walked across the meadow to the cow.

"Cow, PLEASE give me a saucer of milk for the cat," she said, "because unless you do

"Cat    won't  kill   rat,    Rat    won't  gnaw   rope;
Rope won't choke butcher,  Butcher won't kill    ox;
Ox    won't drink water,  Water won't quench fire;
Fire   won't burn stick,  Stick won't beat   dog;
Dog won't bite  pig,  Pig    won't  jump  stile;  And  I shan't get home 'til  morn-ing."

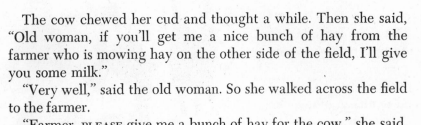

The cow chewed her cud and thought a while. Then she said, "Old woman, if you'll get me a nice bunch of hay from the farmer who is mowing hay on the other side of the field, I'll give you some milk."

"Very well," said the old woman. So she walked across the field to the farmer.

"Farmer, PLEASE give me a bunch of hay for the cow," she said.

"Old woman," said the farmer, "I'm very thirsty. If you will fetch me a bucket of water from the spring, I'll give you some hay."

"Very well," said the old woman. When she got to the spring, she found the bucket full of holes. Not to be outdone, she covered the bottom of the bucket with pebbles, so it would hold water. Then she carried the bucket of cool water to the thirsty farmer.

As soon as he had finished drinking, he gave her a bunch of hay, and away she went to give it to the cow. As soon as the cow had eaten the hay, she gave the old woman a saucer of milk, and away she went to give it to the cat.

As soon as the cat had drunk the milk

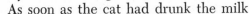

The cat be-gan to kill the rat, The rat be-gan to gnaw the rope;
The rope be-gan to choke the butcher, The butcher be-gan to kill the ox;
The ox be-gan to drink the water, The water be-gan to quench the fire;
The fire be-gan to burn the stick, The stick be-gan to beat the dog;
The dog be-gan to bite the pig, The pig be-gan to jump the stile;

And so she got home be-fore morn-ing!

Chestney

# The Fox Jumped Up

TRADITIONAL ENGLISH NURSERY SONG

The fox jump'd up in a hun-gry plight, And begg'd the moon to give him light; For he had ma-ny miles to trot that night, Be - fore he reach'd his den, O, den, O, den, O; For he had ma-ny miles to trot that night, Be - fore he reach'd his den, O.

2. At last he came to the old farmyard,
Where the ducks and geese declared 'twas hard
That their nerves should be shaken,
   and their rest disturbed,
By a visit from Mr. Fox O.

3. He took the grey duck by the neck,
And swung it right across his back;
Said he, "By good luck,
   here's a good fat duck,
So I'll be off to my den, O."

4. Old Mrs. Slipper Slopper jumped out of bed,
And out of the window popped her head;
"Oh, John, John, John,
   the grey goose is gone!
And the fox is off to his den, O!"

5. John went up to the top of the hill,
And blew a blast both loud and shrill.
Said the fox, "That's very pretty
   music; still,
I'd rather be in my den, O."

6. At last the fox got to his den,
To his dear little foxes eight, nine, ten;
Said he, "By good luck,
   here's a good fat duck,
With his legs all dangling down, O."

7. He sat down to dinner with a hungry wife,
They did very well without fork or knife;
They never ate a better duck
   in all their life,
And the little ones fought for the bones, O.

# Chicken Licken

WORDS FROM AN OLD NURSERY TALE
MUSIC BY MARY JARMAN NELSON

*Verse* 1. As Chick-en Lick-en, so 'tis said, Went out one day a-call-in', An
*Refrain.* "No way to stop it I can see, And 'tis a dread-ful thing, "Oh!" No

a-corn dropped up-on her head. Said she: "The sky is fall-ing."
mat-ter what be-comes of me, I'll go and tell the king, "Oh!"

Chestney

2. Said Henny Penny, "Wait for me,
   We two will go a-calling."
   "Oh no, dear Henny Penny, see!
   The big blue sky is falling."
   REFRAIN: "No way to stop it . . .

3. Said Ducky Lucky, "Wait for me,
   We three will go a-calling."
   "Oh no, dear Ducky Lucky, see!
   The big blue sky is falling."
   REFRAIN: "No way to stop it . . .

4. Said Turkey Lurkey, "Wait for me,
   We four will go a-calling."
   "Oh no, dear Turkey Lurkey, see!
   The big blue sky is falling."
   REFRAIN: "No way to stop it . . .

5. They hurried then to tell the King
   The big blue sky was falling.
   They did not stop for anything,
   Nor did they go a-calling.
   REFRAIN: "No way to stop it . . .

# One More River

FOLK SONG FROM THE OZARKS

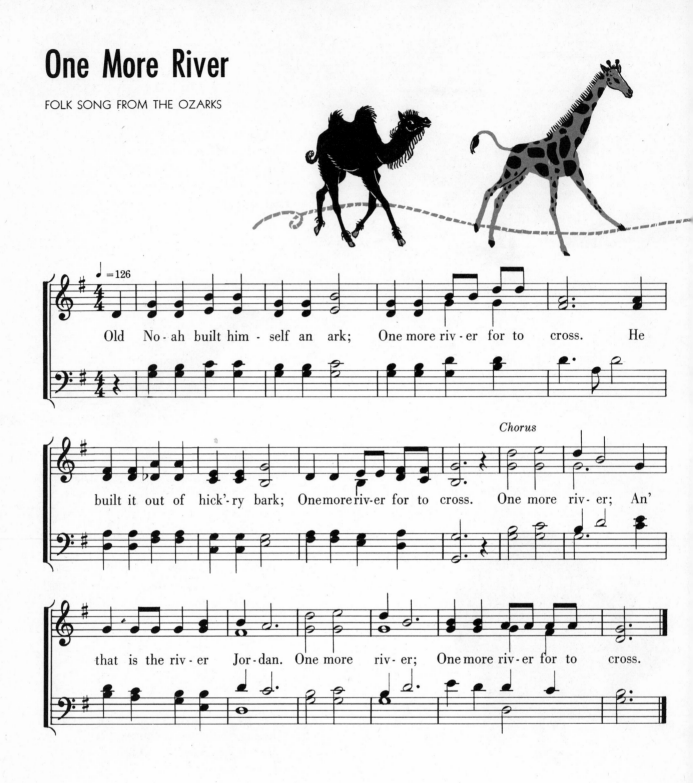

♩ = 126

Old No-ah built him-self an ark; One more riv-er for to cross. He
built it out of hick'-ry bark; One more riv-er for to cross. One more riv-er; An'
that is the riv-er Jor-dan. One more riv-er; One more riv-er for to cross.

*Chorus*

The animals went in two by two,
The elephant a-leanin' on the kangaroo.

The animals went in three by three,
Polecat a-talkin' to the bumblebee.

The animals went in four by four,
Old Noah got mad and hollered for more.

The animals went in five by five,
Old Noah hollered, "You look alive."

The animals went in six by six,
The hyena laughing at the monkey's tricks.

The animals went in seven by seven,
Says the ant to the elephant, "Who are you shovin'?"

The animals went in ten by ten,
Old Noah blowed his whistle then.

Then the voyage did begin,
Old Noah pulled his gangplank in.

They never knowed where they was at,
Till the old ark bumped on Ararat.

chestney

# Tree in the Woods

FOLK SONG AS SUNG IN GEORGIA

1. Down in the woods, there was a tree; The pret-tiest lit-tle
2. And on the tree, there was a limb; The pret-tiest lit-tle

tree  you ev-er did  see. Tree in the ground, (*Repeat*
limb  you ev-er did  see. Limb on the tree,  and the

*as needed*)  And the green grass grew all  a - round.
tree  in the ground, And the green grass grew all  a - round.

3. And on that limb, there was a branch;
   The prettiest little branch you ever did see.
   Branch on the limb,
   And the limb on the tree,
   And the tree in the ground,
   And the green grass grew all around.

4. And on that branch, there were some twigs;

5. And on those twigs, there was a nest;

6. And in that nest, there was an egg;

7. And on that egg, there was a speck;

*Chestney*

# The Gingerbread Man

FOLK TALE ARRANGED BY MARY JARMAN NELSON

One day a little old woman was baking gingerbread. She decided to make some of the dough into a gingerbread man. She gave him a funny pointed hat with a cherry on top of it, and a jacket with cloves for buttons. After the bread had baked a while, she opened the oven door and out jumped the gingerbread man. He skipped about the room, then ran through the door singing:

"Run, run, run, As fast as you can; You can't catch me, I'm the gin-ger bread man!"

The little old lady ran as fast as she could, but she couldn't catch him.

The little old man was planting some peas in the garden. He saw the gingerbread man and the little old lady running after him. So the little old man dropped his hoe and started running too. But the gingerbread man just laughed and sang:

*"Run, run, run, as fast as you can. You can't catch me, I'm the gingerbread man!"*

He ran down the road and across the field where some men were cutting hay. They all dropped their scythes and started running. But the gingerbread man just laughed and sang:

*"Run, run, run, as fast as you can. You can't catch me, I'm the gingerbread man!"*

They all ran as fast as they could, but no one could catch him. On and on ran the gingerbread man. Presently he came to a barn where some men were threshing wheat. They dropped their flails and started running after him. But the gingerbread man just laughed and sang:

*"Run, run, run, as fast as you can. You can't catch me, I'm the gingerbread man!"*

93

After a while the gingerbread man ran past an old red cow in a pasture, who was chewing her cud. When she saw him she stopped chewing and started after him. But the gingerbread man just laughed and sang:

*"Run, run, run, as fast as you can. You can't catch me, I'm the gingerbread man!"*

He ran and ran until he came to a forest. While he was resting under a tree, he saw a sly old fox, who looked as though he were asleep. So the gingerbread man tickled the end of the fox's nose and sang:

*"Run, run, run, as fast as you can. You can't catch me, I'm the gingerbread man!"*

But the sly old fox was not asleep, and before you could say "Jack Robinson" he had gobbled up the gingerbread man's funny pointed hat. This frightened the gingerbread man so badly that he started running twice as fast. He left the sly old fox far behind, and for all I know he is still running and singing his song:

*"Run, run, run, as fast as you can. You can't catch me, I'm the gingerbread man!"*

Chestney

## CHAPTER SEVEN

Courtesy John Gass

## SUITING WORD TO DEED

Your school may celebrate many occasions not marked in red on the calendar, such as Parents Day, or a rally for the football team. These are the days for our pre-schooler to be part of his whole school. He is often more excited by these events than his more sophisticated brothers and sisters in high school.

Songs there are aplenty for Christmas, Easter, or patriotic holidays. "But where," says the classroom teacher, "can I find a song for football day?"

"To - day's the first of May."

"To - day is foot-ball day."

Here's the answer. If a song is not available it can be made. With a little help, the children themselves can suit the word to the occasion. They begin by making simple substitutions, such as "Mary had a little ball," instead of "lamb." "Let's sing the way it looks," the teacher says. "It is round and blue," some child replies.

In encouraging the making of an endless repertoire, the teacher remembers that words are more easily sung if they fit the tune. New words are checked with old, to make sure the accented word or syllable is fitted to the note right after the bar line. (The bar line in music always tells us where the accent comes.)

Using the first song in this chapter, how many days can we celebrate?

"To -|day is Christ-mas | day."

"To -|day is New Year's | Day."

"To -|day is Pa- rents | Day."

"To -|day's a rain- y | day."

"My |birth- day is to- | day."

# SPECIAL OCCASIONS

The red-combed rooster that lives in the big pen in the kindergarten room crowed lustily. John eyed the visitor to see if Tonto's efforts impressed him properly. They didn't; so John ambled over and tugged at the visitor's sleeve. "Mister, that means it's fifteen minutes after."

"Indeed," said the visitor, looking at his watch, which registered 10:47.

Miss T. explained that the children had gotten the idea that Tonto crowed every fifteen minutes, and that each crow was celebrated as if the clock had struck.

Our little people are like that about many of their special occasions. Celebrate we must, with proper vigor and enthusiasm, even though they do not fully understand what it is all about. Christmas means Santa and presents; Easter brings eggs and the Easter bunny; Thanksgiving is synonymous with turkey. Birthdays mean cake and, also, "Now I am really getting big." And to the teacher, these birthdays, each carefully celebrated, come as a reminder: "We are indeed very young. Meaning will come with time."

# Today's the First of May

ENGLISH FOLK SONG

*This handy song might even be used on May 1, with gay crepe paper Maypole streamers flying; or as children put flowers into the May baskets they have made to hang on mother's door.*

1. To - day's the first of May, To - day's the first of May, May, May; To -
2. Good - bye, fare - well, my friend, We'll meet a - gain some day, some day; We'll

day's the first of May, To - day's the first of May.
meet a - gain some day, Be - fore the first of May.

# Birthday Song

WORDS AND MUSIC BY LILLIAN E. WILLSE

*A birthday song that doesn't mention the individual's name just doesn't do justice to the occasion. Miss T. lets the honor child choose a game. You'll have your own verse and way to celebrate.*

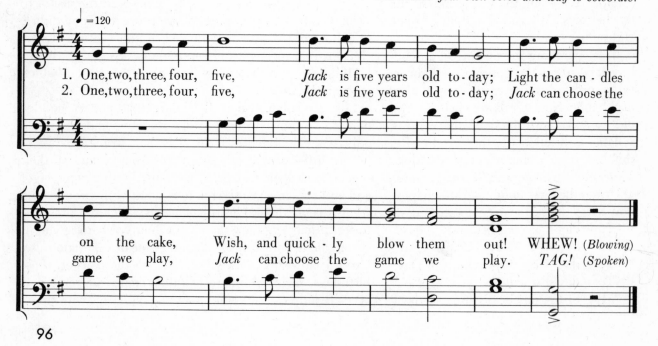

1. One, two, three, four, five, Jack is five years old to - day; Light the can - dles
2. One, two, three, four, five, Jack is five years old to - day; Jack can choose the

on the cake, Wish, and quick - ly blow them out! WHEW! *(Blowing)*
game we play, Jack can choose the game we play. TAG! *(Spoken)*

96

*Halloween—favorite holiday of our little people!*
*If only teacher, too, could hide behind a mask*
*until the excitement has subsided a bit.*

# Halloween Mask

WORDS AND MUSIC BY ELIZABETH GRENOBLE

Who am I be-hind this mask, With nose so big, and whisk-ers too?

Who am I be-hind this mask, Who is it that is ask-ing you?

# The Witch Rides

WORDS AND MUSIC BY GRACE M. MESERVE

The witch is on her broom-stick, Rid-ing ve-ry fast._____

Oo,_____ Oo,_____ Hal-low-e'en at last!_____

# Halloween Fun

WORDS AND MUSIC BY
ANNA MARY MEALAND

*Witches may ride away but Jack O' Lantern, symbol of the day, remains.*

1. Out in the field — where the corn - stalks lie, Some
2. Scoop out the mid - dle and cut a hat, We'll

pump - kins are sleep - ing but by and by, We'll
make eyes and nos - es, Just think of that! We'll

pick them and bring them, — one by one,
put in a can - dle to shine right through, And

In - to the house for Hal - low - e'en fun.
now — they're Jack - 'O - Lan - terns; Boo!

98

*The emphasis is on the turkey and trimmings, of course; but even little children can sense the quiet moment before the feast—of grace before meat.*

# Thanksgiving

WORDS AND MUSIC BY ALICE E. WORKMAN

Thanks - giv - ing, Thanks - giv - ing, Thanks giv - ing's al - most here!
Thanks - giv - ing, Thanks - giv - ing, The fam - ily gath - ers near.

*Just the same, it's fun to whet up the appetite. A change of menu is in order to suit the plans being made in individual homes.*

# Guess!

WORDS AND MUSIC BY BILLY HOWARD (AGED 9)

Tur - key, dump - lings, peas, boiled on - ions; Pea - nuts, chick - en,

pump - kin pie; See if you can guess what day this is! ___

*"Who wants to be a duck? Who'd rather be a turkey?" At Thanksgiving time, Miss T.'s room is full of barnyard fowls, "gobbles" and "quacks."*

# Ducks and Turkeys

WORDS AND MUSIC BY GRACE M. MESERVE

♩ =44

Gob - ble, gob - ble, gob - ble, gob - ble! Quack! Quack! Quack!

Tur - keys al - ways gob - ble, But ducks go "Quack!"

# Church Songs

People look upward, all over the world, and render praise and thanksgiving to their God. Our little people have no prejudices they have not picked up from adults.

*As sung in India. Translated literally, the words are "God, His name is truth."*

## Mohammedan Beggar's Song

Al - lah Ka nam hay___ su-ch-cha.

## Hindu Hymn

A - go Ra - ma ho___ Ra - ma.

*As heard in India by an American who spent his life there. The words mean "He is God."*

## Sh'Ma Yisroel

*The words of this prayer from the Jewish liturgy are so sacred they may be sung only in Hebrew,— "Hear, O Israel, the Lord is God."*

Sh'ma Yis - ro - el, A - do - noi E - lo - hey - nu, A - do - noi ___ e - had.

## When the Saints Go Marching By

*This Negro spiritual has been widely sung by many Americans, both in and out of church.*

Oh, when the Saints, Go march-ing by, Oh when the Saints go march-ing by; Oh Lord I want to be in their num-ber,___ When the Saints go march-ing by.___

*Differences can be matters of interest and respect; many of them need not be reconciled. This is an attitude which can be emulated, too, by our children, when it is presented to them.*

## Saint Catherine

*This is the refrain, only, of a hymn that is frequently sung in both Protestant and Catholic churches. Words are by Frederick W. Farber; music by Henri F. Hemy and James G. Walton.*

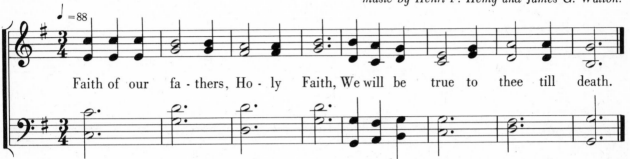

Faith of our fa - thers, Ho - ly Faith, We will be true to thee till death.

*This old Sunday School song is one of the favorite songs of childhood. The words are by Anna B. Warner; the music by William B. Bradbury. Children can play it on the piano. (See pages 74-6.)*

## Jesus Loves Me

1. Je - sus loves me! this I know, For the Bi - ble tells me so;
2. Je - sus loves me! He will stay Close be - side me all the way;

Lit - tle ones to Him be - long; They are weak, but He is strong. Yes, Je - sus
If I love Him, when I die, He will take me home on high.

*Refrain*

loves me! Yes, Je - sus loves me! Yes, Je - sus loves me! The Bi - ble tells me so.

# Song for Hanukah

JEWISH FOLK SONG

Ha-nu-kah, Ha-nu-kah, what a hap-py time!___ Tops spin round, can-dles burn, fami-lies gath-er round;___ Ha-nu-kah, Ha-nu-kah, let us dance and sing,___ Can-dles burn, Guests come in, pre-sents they will bring.

*This Negro spiritual tells the Christmas story so simply that even little children can understand, even though they will not grasp the full significance of the day.*

# Mary Had a Baby, Yes, Lord

AMERICAN NEGRO SPIRITUAL

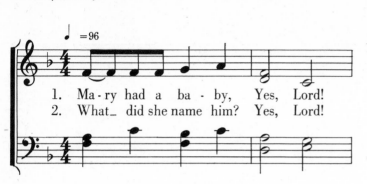

♩ = 96

1. Ma-ry had a ba-by,   Yes, Lord!
2. What_ did she name him?   Yes, Lord!

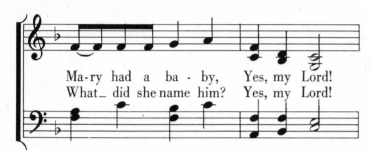

Ma-ry had a ba-by,   Yes, my Lord!
What_ did she name him?   Yes, my Lord!

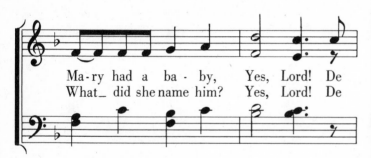

Ma-ry had a ba-by,   Yes, Lord! De
What_ did she name him?   Yes, Lord! De

peo-ple keep a-com-in' an' de train done gone.
peo-ple keep a-com-in' an' de train done gone.

3. She named him King Jesus,
   She named him King Jesus, Lord!

4. Where was he born? Yes, Lord,
   Where was he born? Yes, my Lord!

5. Born in a manger, Yes, Lord,
   Born in a manger, Yes, my Lord!

# Round the Christmas Tree

MEXICAN FOLK SONG

*Gaily our children dance around their Christmas tree with its brightly colored balls and lights, and mysterious packages.*

1. We are gai - ly sing - ing,
2. We are gai - ly sing - ing,

'round the Christ-mas tree, Sing a song for
'round the Christ-mas tree, Sing a song for

Christ-mas, Christ-mas Day is near.
San - ta, San - ta will be here.

*Chorus*

La la la, la la la, la la la la la la la,

La la la, la la la, la la la la la la la.

104

# I Saw Three Ships

TRADITIONAL ENGLISH CAROL

♩. = 76

1. I saw three ships come sail-ing by, Sail-ing by, sail-ing by, I
2. And what d'you think was in them then, In them then, in them then, And
3. Three pret-ty girls were in them then, In them then, in them then, Three

saw three ships come sail-ing by, On Chri-si-mas Day in the morn - ing.
what d'you think was in them then, On Chri-si-mas Day in the morn - ing?
pret-ty girls were in them then, On Chri-si-mas Day in the morn - ing.

## Santa's Sleigh

WORDS AND MUSIC BY GRACE M. MESERVE

♩ = 88

1. Jin - gle, jin - gle, lit - tle bells, On old San - ta's sleigh.
2. Jin - gle, jin - gle, lit - tle bells, What have you for me?

Jin - gle, jin - gle, lit - tle bells, San - ta's on his way.
"Toys and books and pret - ty things, For your Christ-mas tree."

105

## In a Manger

WORDS AND MUSIC BY ELOISE LISLE JOHNSON

*There is a place, too, for new Christmas carols, written especially for little children to sing and enjoy during the holiday period.*

In a man-ger far a-way,

Slept a ti-ny babe. Lit-tle Je-sus, whom we love, In a man-ger lay.

## America

WORDS BY SAMUEL FRANCIS SMITH
MUSIC BY HENRY CAREY

*The whole school is busy with celebrations of patriotic holidays. Our pre-schoolers will want to sing the national favorites along with older sisters and brothers, on these days.*

1. My coun-try! 'tis of thee, Sweet land of lib-er-ty,
2. Our fa-thers' God, to Thee, Au-thor of lib-er-ty,

Of thee I sing; Land where my fa-thers died, Land of the
To Thee we sing; Long may our land be bright With Free-dom's

Pil-grims' pride, From ev-'ry_ moun-tain side Let_ free-dom ring.
ho-ly light; Pro-tect_ us_ by Thy might, Great_ God, our King.

*One school—one community—one country, and the hope that within their lifetimes our little people may come to live in one world.*

## America, the Beautiful

WORDS BY KATHERINE LEE BATES
MUSIC BY SAMUEL A. WARD

O beau-ti-ful for spa-cious skies, For am-ber waves of grain,_ For pur-ple moun-tain maj-es-ties A-bove the fruit-ed plain._ A-mer-i-ca! A-mer-i-ca! God shed His grace on thee,_ And crown thy good with broth-er-hood From sea to shin-ing sea.

# Valentine's Day

WORDS AND MUSIC BY LOLLY WILLIAMS

*This Valentine message is not particularly novel; but has anyone ever thought of a better one?*

♩. = 84

1. Oh, I re-ceived a val-en-tine, All sil-ver-y and red.___ I can-not guess who
2. To-day I sent a val-en-tine, A pret-ty lit-tle note. They'll ne-ver guess who

sent it 'Cause this is all it said: "I love you. Guess who? I love you. Guess who?___
sent it 'Cause this is all I wrote: "I love you. Guess who? I love you. Guess who?___

# Pretty Easter Bunny

WORDS AND MUSIC BY ANGELA WIECHARD

*And then comes springtime and Easter, bringing colored eggs, and bunnies and—for the little ladies—a new dress.*

♩ = 88

Pret-ty East-er Bun-ny, Oh! what hap-pi-ness you bring.

Come! East-er Bun-ny, Come and tell us it is spring.

108

## CHAPTER EIGHT

## WHOSE KINDERGARTEN?

Just as Miss T. and her children are frequently seen here and there throughout town, making rich use of all the resources of the community, so the people of Miss T.'s town are frequently seen in her classroom.

The carpenter drops off an empty nail keg, as he rattles by, so that the children may have another drum. The rug manufacturer brings samples, for the Doll House, when he comes to talk to upper grades. Pictures cut from magazines, records of which people are tired, colorful dresses for the costume box all come in; brought by people who come to help on the playground, help with wraps in winter; come to bring talents, such as telling stories or playing an instrument.

How do all these people in the community know what Miss T. needs? When she meets them in their clubs, in their homes, she does not hesitate to tell them. Miss T. believes that her kindergarten belongs not to her, but to the town; that her successes or failures there in making good citizens are of public concern. As a result, people in town are proud of their kindergarten and glad to help.

The carpenter always stops to play a drum; the mother who brings pictures for Tales with Tunes stays to hold up the picture at the right place. At PTA meeting Miss T. has the mothers sing "John the Rabbit" and waggle their hands over their heads, just as the children do. "How can they take care of their half of the kindergarten program at home, if they don't know what goes on at school?"

Courtesy John Gass

# HOME AND COMMUNITY

"May we keep Sara for lunch? She and Doris have been singing and swinging all morning. She's got Doris carrying a tune. Sara's wonderful, Madeline; how *have* you done it?"

Thoughtfully, Madeline hung up and went back to her ironing. Sara was a nice child . . . and musical. Helen was right. She pondered. . . . Had she and Timmy *done* anything?

Well, they'd been happy and had expressed that happiness in song. Many of their jokes had been sung back and forth from living room to kitchen. Unconsciously she hummed one of their favorite tunes. She was glad they'd kept the old piano; even when the television set came in.

"That piano just ruins the room," Helen had said.

Sara had climbed up on the bench beside her when she was less than three. Nowadays she could play along on one note, when they all sang some of the old songs together.

She and Timmy would see that Sara had piano lessons. Not yet. Miss T. had advised them to wait. They'd get her a set of tonal blocks for Christmas. Perhaps she'd be able to play the birthday tune in time for daddy's birthday. . . .

# Oh! Susanna

WORDS AND MUSIC BY STEPHEN C. FOSTER

*Written in 1846, as Foster steamboated down the Ohio on one of the boats plying between Pittsburgh and New Orleans, this song became the favorite marching song of the pioneers.*

1. I_____ came from Al - a - bam - a With my ban - jo on my
2. It_____ rained all night the day I left, The weath - er it was

knee, I'm_____ goin' to Loui - si - an - a My_____
dry; The_____ sun so hot I froze to death; Su -

true love for to see;
san - na, don't you cry.

Oh, Su - san - na! Oh, don't you cry for me, I've_____

come from Al - a - bam - a With my ban - jo on my knee.

110

WORDS TRADITIONAL
MUSIC BY EDWARD L. WHITE

# Billy Boy

*One page could not hold all the verses your chil-
dren will want to sing to this, their favorite song.
"How old is she?" is generally the favorite. You'll
be in trouble if that one is left out.*

Oh,— where have you been, Bil-ly Boy, Bil-ly Boy, Oh,— where — have you been, charm-ing Bil-ly? I have been to seek a wife, She's the joy— of my life, She's a young thing and can-not leave her moth-er.—

2. Did she bid you to come in, Billy Boy, Billy Boy?
   Yes, she bid me to come in; there's a dimple in her chin.

3. Did she take your hat, Billy Boy, Billy Boy?
   Yes, she took my hat; but she threw it at the cat.

4. Did she give you a chair, Billy Boy, Billy Boy?
   Yes, she gave me a chair; but there was no bottom there.

5. How old is she, Billy Boy, Billy Boy?
   Three times six and four times seven; twenty-eight and eleven.

6. Can she make a cherry pie, Billy Boy, Billy Boy?
   She can make a cherry pie; quick as a cat can wink her eye.

7. Can she milk a mulie cow, Billy Boy, Billy Boy?
   She can milk a mulie cow; if her Mammy shows her how.

# Everybody's Welcome

RELIGIOUS FOLK SONG
OF THE TENNESSEE HILL COUNTRY

*Many of these songs of the old camp ground, sung at revival meetings, were constructed around a "family word." The song was stretched to many verses by using, successively, "fathers," "mothers," "sisters," "brothers," "children."*

Ev'-ry-bo-dy's wel-come,— Yes, yes, wel-come! Ev'-ry-bo-dy's wel-come,—

Come a-long and go. Oh, glo-ry! Hal-le-lu-jah! Oh, glo-ry! Come a-long and go.

# Down in the Valley

AMERICAN FOLK SONG

*This is the best-loved of the "lonesome tunes" of the Kentucky mountains. As Carl Sandburg remarks in his "The American Songbag," "it is full of wishes—and dances a little—and hopes a beloved dancing partner will come back."*

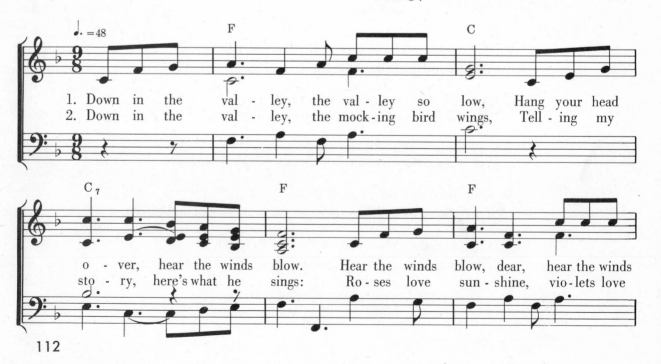

1. Down in the val - ley, the val - ley so low, Hang your head
2. Down in the val - ley, the mock-ing bird wings, Tell - ing my

o - ver, hear the winds blow. Hear the winds blow, dear, hear the winds
sto - ry, here's what he sings: Ro - ses love sun - shine, vio-lets love

blow,      Hang your head    o - ver,    hear the winds    blow.
dew,      An - gels in    heav - en    knows I love    you.

*Songs traveled with the people, as early Americans spread over the land. This old Negro spiritual "When the Chariot Comes," was taken up to the mountains, and its words changed, accordingly. (Your child can help play this one. See page 76.)*

## She'll Be Comin' Round the Mountain

AMERICAN FOLK SONG

1. She'll be com-in' round the moun-tain, When she comes. ___ She'll be com-in' round the moun-tain, When she comes. ___ She'll be com-in' round the moun-tain, She'll be com-in' round the moun-tain, She'll be com-in' round the moun-tain, When she comes. ___

2. She'll be drivin' six white horses,
    When she comes.
She'll be drivin' six white horses,
She'll be drivin' six white horses,
She'll be drivin' six white horses,
    When she comes.

3. Oh we'll all go to meet her,
    When she comes.
We will kill the old red rooster,
We will kill the old red rooster,
And we'll all have chicken and dumplin',
    When she comes.

113

# Marching Song of the Shepherds

SLOVAK FOLK SONG
TRANSLATED BY MARION BERGMAN

*This song retells a Slovakian folk tale about the shepherds who played their fiddles and bagpipes, on their way to visit the Christ-child. Listen to the chorus; you can hear these instruments.*

1. Shep-herds, leave your flocks to-night, Fol-low yon-der star so bright;
Heark-en to the an-gels' words, Rise and leave your flocks and herds.
2. In a man-ger low He lies, Prais-es ech-o through the skies.
Shep-herds, now your fid-dles play, On your bag-pipes doo-dle gay.

Hai-dom, hai-dom, tid-li-dom, Hai-dom, hai-dom, tid-li-dom.

# Silent Night

WORDS BY JOSEPH MOHR
MUSIC BY FRANZ GRUBER

*High in the Austrian Tyrol, a tired pastor, trudg-ing through the snow on a sick call, looked up at the stars and wrote these words. They were set by his church organist and first sung to the strumming of a guitar, since the organ was broken.*

Si-lent night, ho-ly night, All is calm, all is bright Round yon Vir-gin
Ho-ly In-fant so

Moth-er and Child, ten-der and mild, Sleep in heav-en-ly peace, Sleep in heav-en-ly peace!

114

*Here is a song for rocking, for waving goodbye, for "getting upstairs," for naptime in school, for humming, for strumming on instruments, for living with and enjoying through the years.*

# Goodbye, My Lover

OLD AMERICAN SONG

1. The ship came sail-ing down the bay, Good-bye, my lov-er good-
   heart will ev-er-more be true, Good-bye, my lov-er good-

2. Then cheer up till we meet a-gain, Good-bye, my lov-er good-
   far I roam a-cross the sea, Good-bye, my lov-er good-

bye;___ We may not meet for man-y a day, Good-bye, my lov-er, good-bye.___ My
bye;___ Tho' now we sad-ly say a-dieu, Good-bye, my lov-er, good-bye.___
bye;___ I'll try to bear my wea-ry pain, Good-bye, my lov-er, good-bye.___ Though
bye;___ My ev-'ry thought of you shall be, Good-bye, my lov-er, good-bye.___

*Refrain*

By-low, my ba-by, By-low, my ba-by,

By-low, my ba-by, Good-bye, my lov-er, good-bye!___

115

# The Marines' Hymn

OFFICIAL SONG OF THE
UNITED STATES MARINES

*For nearly one hundred years the Marines' Hymn has been sung around the world, as our Sea Soldiers have faithfully and thrillingly performed their missions for the United States. (Ideas for little soldiers in your home are on pages 74-6.)*

From the Halls of Mon - te - zu - ma To the shores of Trip-o - li; _____ We __ fight our coun-try's bat - tles In the air, on land and sea; _____ First to fight for right and free - dom And to keep our hon-or clean; _____ We are proud to claim the ti - tle Of U - nit - ed States Ma - rine. _____

116

# HELPS FOR THE TEACHER

## FREEDOM WITH INSTRUMENTS

Valuable and necessary as your piano is, you can't take it with you to the playground or carry it to picnics. But there are instruments which give you such freedom; these instruments are both fun to have and to play. Parents as well as teachers will enjoy them, for they can go into the kitchen while dinner is cooking; go to the bedside for a good night song or to entertain a child who is ill. These instruments can go for a Sunday drive, too, with one parent playing a tune as the other drives.

You achieve freedom both for yourself and for your children's musical experiences when you go adventuring with a pipe, ukulele, or autoharp. Your children are busy exploring instruments. Why not you, too? What could make you a more sympathetic and inspiring guide?

If you would share their delight in finding out some simple things about music, try strumming a few simple chords on an autoharp while your children delightedly sing one of their favorite tunes. Listen to the way the words ride high above the accompaniment and the way little voices stand out, sweet and clear. The children can really hear themselves sing; they sing more freely. You'll discover why the troubadours preferred to use strummed instruments as they went about singing their tales of derring-do. What better accompaniment could you find for the songs that come from southern cabins that echoed with the soft sounds of the banjo or guitar? What could be more appropriate for the songs of early days in America, when men took along at least one simple instrument as they trekked across the continent?

Children love to hear a teacher pipe their tunes, too. The pipe is useful for teaching a song if a teacher cannot sing well, or if her voice is tired. Pipes are good to accompany outdoor games; good for guessing games. The teacher pipes a tune and the children guess what it is. The sound of a pipe on the playground also serves to give a child courage to jounce or climb the jungle gym or swing high.

*For information about these instruments, write Peripole Products, Inc., 2917 Avenue R, Brooklyn 29; or Educational Music Bureau, Inc., 30 E. Adams, Chicago 3; or Walberg and Auge, 31 Mercantile St., Worcester 8, Mass.*

### STRUMMING

The autoharp sounds something like the old-fashioned zither. Of all the strumming instruments, it is easiest to play. All you have to do is press down the bar with the proper chord name on it and strum the strings. You can operate the bars and let a child play the strings.

"But how do I know what chords to play and when to play them?"

Throughout the book, songs adapted to strumming have been marked with letters. At the spot marked C, you press down the bar marked C on your autoharp. The clue is given for what and when.

You'll want to go farther than this, however. Start with "Everybody's Welcome," page 112, which is not marked. The basic chord of a key is the I chord. The following chart gives you the letter names of the chords in various keys. You find you want the G bar.

| If the key signature is | | | | | | | |
|---|---|---|---|---|---|---|---|
| The music is in the key of | C | D | E flat | F | G | A | B flat |
| The I chord is | C | D | E flat | F | G | A | B flat |
| The IV chord is | F | G | A flat | B flat | C | D | E flat |
| The V or V7 chord is | G | A | B flat | C | D | E | F |

Now try pressing G at the beginning of every measure. Let your ear tell you if the chord fits, as you sing along. You'll discover it does. What could be simpler? Is this always true? Let's try "One Day One Foot," page 42. Here you'll find that in the next to last measure the G bar doesn't fit. Listen to the tune; doesn't it seem to kick its heels? The chord for action is the V7; try that. When you go back to the G bar, at the last measure, note the nice contrast of action–repose. This is a cadence; like dropping the voice at the close of a sentence. This pattern works many times:

*Mary had a little lamb, little lamb, little lamb,*
I         I         V7         I
*Mary had a little lamb, its fleece was white as snow.*
I         I         V7              I

As you progress, you'll want to experiment with different chords. Don't stick to just those chords charted for you. Use different styles of strumming, too, to suit the character of the music. Soft, languorous music is highly adapted to strumming; but you can get vigorous effects, too. Listen to the recording of "Here Comes the Train." This style of accompaniment helps to stimulate movement.

Simple melody wind instruments are easy to play, inexpensive, and will add much to your own pleasure and to the musical enjoyment of your children. In addition to recorders, which are copies of an old instrument, there are simpler instruments with various trade names: flutophone, tonette, and song flute.

These simpler instruments play the white keys of the piano, also F sharp and B flat. You can play nine tones without overblowing:

You play:                 You hear:
(range)                   (notes sounded)

You can easily play the tunes of these songs:

Rudy, Rudy, Rannie, page 34
Little Wind                     7
April                           7
Little Redbird                  9
I Have a Bonnet                16
Cookies                        17
Two in the Middle              30
Rose, Rose                     32
Song of the Pigs               60

The best keys are C, D, F, and G. You may want to pipe a song that has more black keys, as written for piano, "The Marines' Hymn," for instance, in E flat. The key of D is close to E flat. Try sounding D on the piano and playing the tune by ear. If you aren't successful, you can transpose the song as you read it, by thinking, "Every note is one note lower."

Here are a few hints for beginners:

1. Try to catch the spirit of a tune.

2. Breathe deeply and try to blow with a steady column of air.

3. Use pipes for sound effects—train whistles, bird songs, etc.

4. Play lullabies as well as spirited tunes.

5. Notice the smooth style of phrasing of the flute as it plays "Philippine Lullaby" on the record. You can imitate this style, also that of the clarinet in "Little Wind," and the oboe in "Dolly's Lullaby."

When you pick up a child's rhythm with a drum, in order to emphasize the pattern for the group, you will want to play distinctly and precisely; the sound you make need be neither extremely loud nor vibrant. When, however, you are drumming for a dramatic play, in which a mood is created and sustained, with growing climax and release (as in the play of running in and out of the ocean, with its breathtakingly high waves), you will probably have to wrestle with your inhibitions, during your first few experiences, in order to give a really effective performance. Remember there was nothing politely mincing about the performance of Indians drumming up an excursion upon the warpath. When you can use the drum freely, without inhibition, your children will lose themselves, too, and respond with full, free, unfettered movements. Study the recording of "The Tiger," and note how movement is stimulated by its percussive accompaniment. Note also how the mood is created and sustained through the use of instruments with suitable timbre and the employment of fitting *crescendos* and *decrescendos*.

During the period when group movement is not synchronized, because each child's own pattern is slightly different due to body build and growth factors, the sound of the drum is ideal for accompanying group movement. With the drum, the underbeat can be played without any specific metric accents. Thus everyone is motivated but no one is forced into a pattern for which he is not ready. Remember that little children do not have enough control to move slowly. Be prepared for movement faster than you indicate. Don't be concerned if children sing in one rhythm and move in another. Tempos should be carefully considered, however, when songs are sung, apart from body movement. There is a tempo at which any given piece of music sounds best. Metronome marks are given for all songs in this book. If you remember that 60 represents one beat a second, and use this as a reference point, you will not find it difficult to approximate tempos.

You can add much to the enjoyment and richness of your children's music through the use of percussion instruments. Fortunately the media for drumming are practically endless—running all the way from everyday things with interesting sounds to precision-made marimbas and diatonic and chromatic bells. Most of your percussion instruments are non-pitched instruments. Some percussions do play pitches, such as marimbas and bells. You might also like to experiment with water-tuned bottles and glasses, which are fun to make.

Drums and other percussion instruments are useful for sound effects during dramatic play. Take, for instance, "Here Comes the Train," page 22. After children have developed a reproductive play, numerous sound effects are added with sandblocks, bells, reiterated chords on a chording instrument, etc. Listen to the recording of this song to see how percussion and other sound effects have been used to simulate actual sounds in the child's environment.

Pitched percussion instruments are easy to play and make excellent melody instruments. For persons of limited musical backgrounds they offer a simple means of learning tunes.

Interesting accompaniments can be worked out with pitched percussion instruments. Listen to the music box effect of the celesta in the recordings of "Dance Thumbkin" and "Little Marionettes." Try to duplicate this effect on your bells.

Pitched percussion instruments are also good for sound effects. Take, for example, "The Woodpecker," page 6. Sing the song and play E or B, or both, throughout, with a steady recurring beat. You will hear this interesting effect when you play the recording of the song.

MARY JARMAN NELSON

118

# Improvisation at the Piano

BY NORMAN LLOYD

Improvisation is of paramount importance to the pre-school teacher. She will always have the music she needs to meet a situation that arises, if she can "create" it, on the spot. Any teacher who has some technical ability at the piano can improvise. Both finger dexterity and musicianship will increase, if she follows the "hints" presented here. All of the material has been written with movement in mind, since "rhythms" is an important area in pre-school. The music has been kept simple, so the teacher can watch her class. In general:

1. Be courageous. Don't be restrained by ideas of "correctness" or "voice-leading." As long as you keep things moving, rhythmically, you are all right. If you can't resolve a dissonance, make it, or any other unwanted idea, a basic part of your improvisation.

2. Don't be afraid of any strange or unusual sounds that you discover as you improvise dramatic or descriptive music. Low growling "clusters" of tone might be just the right thing for a "bear-walk." Often the "wild" sounds are more effective than usual sounds.

3. Don't feel unsuccessful if an idea does not come out just as you wanted, or doesn't evolve into a fine piece of music; improvisation differs from composition in that once a musical idea is played, it cannot be altered. The composer has a chance to think about his music and perfect it, after his first draft.

4. Give your children a chance to improvise. One child may play a scale-tune while another plays a drum beat. This can provide an exciting accompaniment to movement undertaken by the rest of your class.

5. Experiment and add musical ideas to your repertoire. As you listen to music, or read through music, try to analyze how the composer achieves his effect. Take a measure from some piece of music and see if you can make a different piece based on this measure. Try taking the left-hand accompaniment to a folk song and make up a "new" tune. Adopt the motto "I wonder what will happen if . . ." and put it into musical practice.

6. Always try to bear in mind that music takes place in time. Try to make your music flow phrasewise, rather than measure by measure. Feel the impetus in a phrase and the relation of phrase to phrase, as the music goes along.

BUT COME, LET'S IMPROVISE. You don't know traditional harmony? You don't need to. We begin with the melodic and rhythmic elements of music. Place the thumb of the right hand on C and the fifth finger on G. Start on C, E, or G and, having decided on a meter, let the melody run along scalewise, with the rhythmic pulse carrying you along until you feel you are at the end of a phrase. Try to end on C, E, or G; but if you land on another note, call it a semi-cadence and start over again, with C, E, or G your eventual objective. Be sure that your melodies are not aimless or formless, and try to give each phrase a contour. Play in various tempos, with different dynamics.

I   For convenience in reading, the following examples are written for the center of the keyboard; play them higher or lower, in different octaves, so that you hear the effect of the different registers. If you skip around inside the fifth, make this skip an integral part of the melody, not just an arbitrary movement of tone.

In relating these melodic ideas to movement, note that *b* and *c* could be used for marching; *d* is a waltz which could be used for "skating" or swinging movements; *e* for running or skipping; *f* introduces the first black key and, if played at a moderate rate of speed, suggests a smooth walk; *g*, played staccato, suggests jumps and leaps. Note the compositional device of "interval contraction and expansion" in *g* and *h*. Improve on these melodic ideas and expand them. Change the bar line so that the first count becomes an upbeat, and note the change in emphasis in the melody.

II   For variety, and as a method of extension, move your hand to another fifth:

119

**III** Use the same fifths in each hand and, while the right hand plays a melody, let the left hand accent the important rhythmic spots. In *a* and *b,* the left hand plays a "drone" bass; in *c* and *d,* the left hand plays the notes of the fifth alternately; in *e,* the left hand repeats one note to give a meter of three:

**IV** Change the fifths and experiment with key changes to correspond to the changing fifth. (The lower note of the fifth will be the keynote.)

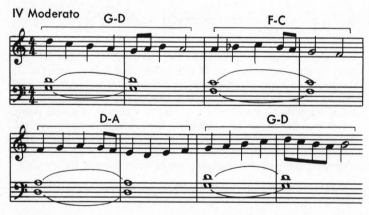

**V** For more motion and a little variety, add the neighboring tone above the fifth in the left hand. Improvise melodies over these patterns:

**VI** THE OSTINATO is a repeated pattern of notes, in any part of the music. It can be very short, as in the first six examples below, or it can become quite complex, as in *g*. For added sonority we can use three-note combinations (triads) against the *ostinato,* just as we used single notes earlier, in melodies. The simplest *ostinato* is that which alternates from scale 8 to scale 5. Get the *ostinato* started and then build a triad on the keynote, using scale 1-3-5. Move your triads against the *ostinato,* and you will have variety and dissonance, which gives added drive to the music. At first use triads as they appear in the scale, then experiment with triads *not* in the scale. In *a, b,* and *c,* the *ostinato* is in the bass part; in *d,* it is in the upper part. When improvising with triads in this fashion, do not think of them as harmonic progressions, but as a single melodic line which is being paralleled.

Fill in the interval from scale 8 to scale 5, as in *e*. Experiment with parallel thirds in the right hand—again treated not as harmonic sounds, but as a melodic line.

VI e

VI f

*Ostinatos* can become complex as at *g* (below). In this case, the right hand will not move as much as in the earlier examples.

VI g

# SCALES AND MODAL MELODIES

Scales other than our usual major and minor scales have been used by musicians from time immemorial. It is important that children hear music outside our own tonic-dominant tonal system from the very beginning of their education in music. Many of the great masterpieces, large and small, of both past and present, can be understood aurally only by familiarity with modal and pentatonic influences.

**VII** PENTATONIC SCALES are just about the most universal of all scale organizations. They lend themselves to improvisation both for their own beauty and for their foreign "flavors." At first, use the black notes of the piano; any of the five may be the key note, so that you have five different forms of pentatonic to work with. Since these five-note pentatonic scales have no half-step intervals, there are no minor seconds, major sevenths, augmented or diminished intervals between any two notes. In the middle and high registers, the whole scale can be played without any jangle of sound, such as would happen if you played a major scale all at once. One could almost say that you cannot play anything that sounds "wrong" in a pentatonic scale. Possibly this is one reason children seem to love to improvise—sometimes *ad nauseam*—in this scale. Of course the obvious starting point is with "Indian" or "Chinese" music (see *VII a* and *b*, at the right). Try using a pentatonic ostinato against melody (*c*).

VII Pentatonic scales:

**VIII** The medieval modes are scale organizations that dropped out of concert music for a while, but are now being used again by contemporary composers. In folk music, the archaic feeling of some songs is due to the modal influence. Each time we sing "Daddy, Be Gay," we are singing modal music.

VII a

VII b

*Play the right hand one or two octaves higher*

VII c

"Daddy Be Gay" is in the Dorian mode. Example *a* (below) presents this mode and a short melody based on that scale. Note the left-hand extension of the fifth to the interval of the octave, by repeating the lower tone above the fifth. Continue this melody in your own way, being sure to end on the keynote:

VIII a Dorian mode

Slowly

121

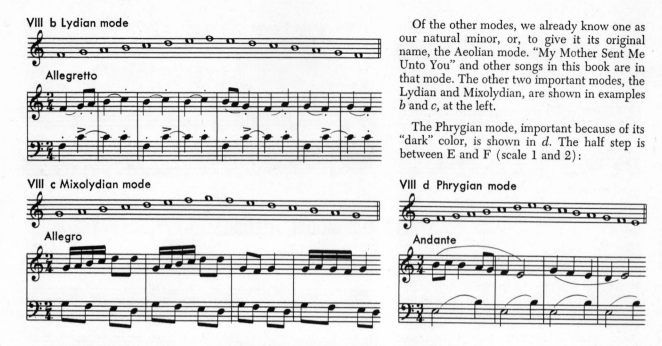

**VIII b Lydian mode**

Allegretto

**VIII c Mixolydian mode**

Allegro

Of the other modes, we already know one as our natural minor, or, to give it its original name, the Aeolian mode. "My Mother Sent Me Unto You" and other songs in this book are in that mode. The other two important modes, the Lydian and Mixolydian, are shown in examples *b* and *c*, at the left.

The Phrygian mode, important because of its "dark" color, is shown in *d*. The half step is between E and F (scale 1 and 2):

**VIII d Phrygian mode**

Andante

# ACCOMPANYING FOR RHYTHMS

**IX a Allegro**

*This symbol means repeat preceding bar*

**IX b Allegro Moderato**

**IX** This discussion has been written with movement in mind, since this is one of the important areas of pre-school teaching.

In playing for movement, it is necessary to be able to "feel" the movement made by the children. Anyone who has seen any of the dances of our Southwest Indians has probably noticed that the drummers perform the dance in miniature as they play their instruments. In our own social dances, the instrumentalists keep their toes touching the floor and bounce on their heels, in time with the music. The difference between a poor and good conductor for ballet is that one "beats time" and the other conducts with a feeling for the flow of the dancers on the stage. So, then, should the teacher play for her children, with a kind of identification with what the children are doing. If the teacher really translates their movement into sound, as though her body were a vessel, the children will respond in a freer fashion.

In playing for "motor" movements (those that move around the floor, as opposed to those done in place, like swaying), it is important to use patterns that put the child on his own, rhythmically. Example *a* could be used for running or any kind of rushing dramatic idea, such as a train. While the left hand uses a simple "see-saw" pattern, the right hand is a bit more complicated, and uses syncopation. Use a non-legato touch for motor movements; it will help you feel the movement in your arms and fingers. Example *b* shows a purely rhythmic idea which builds up through cumulative repetition, seems to arrive someplace (measure 7), and then starts over on a new pitch. It could be used for jumping or leaping movements.

122

**X** HARMONIC USAGE. This study, often called "traditional harmony," is a vast topic. It is touched on, in this discussion, to show how some of the techniques of manipulating tones can be applied.

The three primary chords of each key—those based on the first, fourth, and fifth notes of the scale—will usually suffice to harmonize most of the familiar nursery tunes and the uncomplicated songs composed by a group of children. After you learn how to handle these primary chords and how to manipulate them rhythmically, it is comparatively easy to add more variety to your harmonic palette. Example *a* shows how these primary chords appear in the key of G major; *b* shows them in the bass clef; *c* shows how the same notes can be placed more conveniently for the left hand; *d* uses some of the techniques of "rhythmic agitation" that can be applied. At *e* the chords are opened out for greater sonority. The addition of neighboring tones, as at *f*, gives a feeling of more motion.

In harmonizing a melody, the melody itself often tells you what chord to use, as in the well-known song "Looby Loo":

Try this approach to such tunes as "Silent Night," "Oh! Susanna," and "Mary Had a Little Lamb." In these simple tunes you will find that the chord on scale 1 goes either to IV or V; the chord on scale 4 goes to I or V, and the chord on scale 5 usually goes to I. The harmonies usually change on a strong pulse.

The six examples below show how one can start with just a chord progression and come out with a fairly complex melodic line.

*a.* Here is the basic harmonic progression:

*b.* The right hand plays a simple, slow melody using notes taken from the left-hand chord:

*c.* The melody is embellished with "neighboring tones"—the notes above or below the chord tone in the melody:

*d.* The melody is embellished with other notes of the chord:

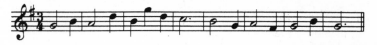

*e.* The melody of *d* is embellished with notes connecting the chord tones. They always move step-wise, and are called "passing tones." The chords in the left hand are in open position:

*f.* The process is reversed in harmonizing a melody. Reduce it to its essential tones and harmonize those tones:

**XI** THIS OLD MAN. Instead of improvising new material, you might want to use an already existing melody and vary it. At the right, are some examples which show how "This Old Man" might be treated.

*a.* Here are the first four measures (plus a few passing tones) with a simple accompaniment:

XI a

*b.* Converted into a dancing, skipping 6/8:

XI b

*c.* In minor and changed in register. After two measures of octaves the left hand plays in thirds below the melody:

XI c

*d.* Here is a little march, using an *ostinato* in the bass:

XI d

*e.* This is a swinging, skating rhythm. The melody is paralleled in triads in the right hand, while the left hand stays on the fifth G-D:

XI e

*f.* Try something like this for jumps; play it an octave lower and feel how ponderous it becomes (elephants, etc.). Use the pedal as indicated:

XI f

There is no limit to how far you can go in the field of improvisation. Once you see the principle by which composers have utilized simple material—putting tone in motion—you will see that there are thousands of ideas to try. Keep trying them!

124

# The Artist Teacher—A Summary

BY GLADYS TIPTON

Of all age groups, young children are probably our most active, most interested, and most persistent music makers. For to them, music is anything that has sound or that possesses rhythmic movement, and, given the opportunity, they search for it and use it instinctively as part and parcel of their daily living. Young children's impromptu music making is, in part, experimental: "How does it sound?" "How does it move?" In part it is an outward expression of feelings too deep for words, or perhaps, simply a confirmation of contentment. And in part, it serves to accompany a rhythmic-dramatic play or work activity.

Intuitive musical gropings of young children are significant, for not only are they inseparably linked to children's all-around growth, but they also represent the beginnings of genuine musical growth.

*1. The artistic teacher frequently tunes in on children's spontaneous music making in order to discover their musical potentialities and preferences.* She realizes that when children are free to "be themselves," musically speaking, their ways of making music will be as individualistic as their ways of moving and speaking and painting. For instance, one child may display a continuing interest in a certain musical activity, while another child may reach out hungrily for every kind of musical experience. Or again, whereas one child may freely sing or dance his deep feelings in vividly imaginative or broadly realistic terms, another child may sing timidly and tentatively, and then when no one is listening.

*2. The artistic teacher encourages much informal individual and small group singing during the day, as a natural part of children's work or play.* She also provides occasional opportunities for the whole group to sing together, regardless of individual singing ability. She realizes that, in the beginning stages, learning to sing is more a matter of free and happy singing throughout each day than a matter of developing precise skills. Thus, as one child begins to sing softly as he paints at his easel, the teacher and children nearby join in the song, singing softly as they work. Or before morning lunch, everyone bows his head and sings grace.

There is no undue alarm at the variations in singing ability that are always present in the average group of young children, for the teacher understands and accepts these individual differences as readily as she accepts their differing abilities in speaking or painting or moving about. In examining basic causes for these wide divergencies in singing, she discovers that lack of experience is usually the most frequent cause, although in some instances certain emotional and physiological disturbances may also have a bearing. And so she threads each day with pleasurable, successful, and extensive opportunities for singing, so that children will learn to sing, *each in his own time.*

Children acquire an easy and flexible use of singing

voices in much the same way that they learn to talk, i.e., by comfortably and freely experimenting, listening, and imitating, in an environment that is literally brimming over with song. In fact, when they are free to do so, they sing themselves through the day. They seldom use singing as an isolated activity, but more often as a vocal accompaniment for rhythmic movement or dramatic play, or as a work chant, or as a part of instrumental exploring. The thoughtful teacher deliberately seeks to expand this kind of vocal-muscular-visual-aural coordination as a part of children's play activity, realizing that the very breadth of this experience insures a better kind of musical growth. The fact is that, far more than vocal techniques of precise skills, young children need time—time for vocal experimenting, time for "play" with different voice qualities and pitches, time for discovering "listening ears," and gradually, later on, time for combining flexible voices and listening ears, so that their singing is "in tune."

There is actually no one correct "child voice." Healthy children usually have healthy voices, possessing a greater range of color than we ordinarily think. They are inclined to use different voices for different occasions. In moments of heightened emotional feeling, for instance, the singing may be vigorous, sometimes covering a narrowly restricted range of perhaps only three or four tones. The excitement of "Jingle Bells" and the hypnotic fervor of a repetitive group chant are examples of this. On the other hand, when a child sings to himself, he usually sings quietly, often wandering casually over a range of an octave or more. In like manner, a group of children singing "Away in a Manger," or any other restful song, will be apt to sing softly and calmly. Free, natural, pleasurable singing is usually the best kind of singing for young children, simply because it permits them to "be themselves" and "to sing how they feel."

*3. The artistic teacher is sensitive to young children's deep and abiding satisfaction in action and plans abundantly for it.* Often young children go into rhythmic action simply to tap and to test their own powers. Sometimes it is for the purpose of expressing deep, inner feelings or merely to let off emotional steam. And sometimes they move with abandon, simply because it "feels good." Whenever a child discovers a new and particularly appealing way of moving, he repeats it again and again, occasionally with such delight that other children cannot resist joining in. And so walking, running, turning, twisting, stretching, bending, jumping, sliding, climbing, stamping, rolling, skipping, going round and round, frequently accompanied by snatches of song made up on the spot, are natural rhythmic movements which every child sooner or later explores for himself.

It is not uncommon for combinations of these natural rhythmic movements to appear after children feel at home with single activities. Running to a sudden stop, a run ending with a long slide, a skip embroidered with whirls,

125

a walk punctuated by stamping or ending in a jump, going round and round then falling down, are favorites.

The expressive movement of children, like their singing, is so closely interwoven with their day-by-day living as to be inseparable from it. And it is from these familiar, everyday experiences that children's rhythmic-dramatic play emerges, at first as simple, direct imitation or impersonation, but gradually assuming the continuity and added characterizations of embryo drama.

Thus one child walks the length of the walking board, hops down the step, then continues his hops until he reaches the next board. He continues this alternating walking-hopping rhythm for some time, finally changing it to a walking-hopping-stamping pattern. On another day, after a circus has been to town, one boy says, "I'll be the elephant. Now who will be the clown?" Obligingly, one of his friends turns a somersault, jumps high in the air and flaps his hands. A little girl, who has been watching, turns into a second clown with a stiff-kneed, stiff-armed strut.

The observant teacher notices that as each child experiments rhythmically, he displays certain rhythmic preferences and tends to develop his own unique movement patterns. She discovers, also, that there are wide variations in the precision and imaginativeness of individual rhythmic responses. But here again, she understands that the best kind of rhythmic development takes place only when each child is permitted to grow rhythmically *in his own good time and in his own particular way*. What does it matter if Johnny's run is momentarily bumbling and awkward, as he reaches out with body and imagination to catch the "feel" of a sea gull in flight? What he is doing is finding himself, rhythmically speaking—something that no one else can do for him—and at this point he needs to be unhurried, unrestricted, and secure in his rhythmic exploring. Conscious striving toward precision comes only after he has made a movement pattern his own.

When the teacher improvises accompaniments for children's expressive rhythmic movement, it is almost like the addition of a third dimension. In this case, the teacher allows the children to establish their own preferred tempo and movement pattern, then, once children are in motion, she adds a percussion instrument accompaniment, or improvises a piano accompaniment to fit the rhythmic activity already under way. This is important, because children's tempos are usually faster than adults'. Thus the teacher must be certain that the accompaniment is not too slow for comfortable, natural movement.

Gradually, children learn to adjust their rhythmic movement to a given musical selection which is played or sung for them. But here again, it is a matter of individual readiness, based upon a child's maturity and experience, rather than a matter of specific "training."

4. *The artistic teacher uses children's natural inclination for experimenting with sound and their tendency toward dynamic rhythmic action as a basis for a gradually developing sequence of musical experiences that is consistently geared to individual growth patterns.* Her responsibility here is to sense the moment when children seem to be ready and waiting for a musical nudge forward. Sometimes it is as simple a thing as letting children move freely from one favorite musical activity into a series of related activities, with the teacher merely serving as property man to provide needed space arrangements and musical equipment. Sometimes it may involve good timing on the part of the teacher, as well as a dip into her musical repertoire, in order to supply appropriate new songs or recordings. And occasionally, it may involve a sort of tentative "survey" as the teacher seeks to discover the musical boundaries within which individual children grow comfortably and yet most effectively.

5. *The artistic teacher consistently develops a variety of simple vocal-auditory-motor-visual associations as a part of children's everyday music making, and always in children's own terms.* Many of the imitative vocal or instrumental sound effects which children voluntarily use to accompany their rhythmic-dramatic play are likely to be realistic pictures of their physical movement of *up and down, high and low*, and the like. Children's voices will almost invariably conform in a rough way to the corresponding upward pattern in the rhythmic-dramatic play of climbing stairs, driving a truck uphill, the take-off of an airplane, reaching up to pull a steam train whistle or to pick ripe apples, or, conversely, the downward pattern of coming down stairs, driving a truck downhill, the landing of an airplane, driving, or the lowering of a crane.

Later on, when children move ponderously and heavily in interpreting low-pitched, "thick," slow music, or when they combine a quick run with a long slide in interpreting a fast piano piece that is punctuated with glissando passages, there is considerable discrimination of *fast and slow, loud and soft, high and low*.

A favorite song with one group was a tonally realistic description of falling autumn leaves. With gaily colored scarves tied around their waists, children liked to sing and dance this song, which meandered leisurely down the scale. One day the teacher held a large set of song bells so that the longer bars were parallel and nearest to the floor. The children took turns playing this familiar, descending tune by ear.

One boy's favorite song was "I'm hiding." A high tone on the piano meant hiding high in a tree, while upon hearing a low tone, children crouched close to the floor. This game was used vocally, later on, the children singing "I'm hiding" at extremes of their vocal ranges.

6. *The artistic teacher provides opportunities for children to explore many easily played percussion, melodic, and strumming instruments.* Children seem to use instruments more freely and with more discrimination when the teacher sets up a number of nooks and crannies in which a few instruments can be arranged attractively and somewhat casually, within easy reach, with space enough for active experimentation and yet with privacy enough to absorb some of the accumulating sound. Many of the instruments should be portable so that children can move them with ease—sometimes for use in conjunction with rhythmic-dramatic play, sometimes for experimental try-outs with other instruments, or sometimes simply to play a chosen instrument in surroundings that seem more suitable at the moment.

Among the instruments that children find especially satisfying are *drums* or *tom toms* of all sizes and shapes, some commercial and some homemade; many of the larger ones equipped with handles. Also gongs suspended from sturdy frames and played with soft beaters; *large bells* hung in order of their pitch: *tiny, tinkling bells* strung on ribbon or webbing, *metal* and *glass* and *wooden bells* hanging from stout cords; *chimes* made from metal pipes; *marimbas* and *xylophones,* some of them small sets of commercial "song bells," and others homemade, of stone or wood or plate glass; *autoharps; maracas* and *rattles; castanets* and *tambourines* and *claves;* and, finally, the usual rhythm instruments that are found in every school. The musical experience is always enriched when children thoughtfully explore these instruments, both singly and in combination, or when they use them to devise appropriate accompaniments for activities.

Large drums of varying pitch and timbre, played with soft beaters, are particularly appealing. Sometimes two or three children become absorbed in joint experimentation, to the point where individual rhythms seem to mesh together. This happened one day when Tony persistently repeated the rhythmic pattern ♫ ♩ ♩ , occasionally altering the tempo, but always maintaining the basic figure. Kay, beating a somewhat smaller Chinese tom tom, nearby, clung to her ♩ ♩ ♩ pattern. For a moment, probably quite by accident, these two rhythmic figures seemed to belong together. Both Tony and Kay laughed, liking what they heard. Then, after considerable wavering, they succeeded in bringing the two rhythmic patterns into focus again for a sustained period.

*7. The artistic teacher realizes that listening ears are as important to children's musical growth as are expressive singing voices, rhythmically moving bodies, and sounding instruments.* With this thought in mind, she not only encourages children to listen more discriminatingly as they, themselves, make music; but she also plans for frequent short intervals of listening to music that is produced by others.

There are any number of times when children listen to a recorded song or to the teacher as she sings a new song, or plays a piece on the piano, before they join in singing or before they begin to move rhythmically. Occasionally a child volunteers to sing or play while others listen attentively. Or sometimes, after singing a lullaby, the teacher plays a similar piece on the phonograph, while children listen quietly. This kind of listening participation is so frequent, in fact, that it escapes our serious attention.

Then, again, there are many opportunities during the day when the teacher might arrange for incidental listening to recorded music or to piano music as a background for other activities. The selection of music is important for such times, for it must be more restful than stimulating.

There are times, too, when the teacher turns to appropriate recorded material for enriching certain rhythmic experiences. For instance, after children have been galloping, trotting, high stepping, and tired ponies, at their own preferred tempos, with the teacher adding instrumental accompaniments from time to time, a short, recorded selection suggestive of the same rhythmic movements might be played. But now the children must adjust themselves to a given tempo and rhythmic pattern.

Sometimes a longer, story record will hold children's undivided attention. *Peter and the Wolf* is such an example. And on certain special occasions, when group feeling runs deep, a happy choice of record will not only speak *for* the children, but will also speak *to* them, in an extremely personal way. This happened when the grotesqueness of clowns, which had occupied one group's attention for days, was caught as the children listened to the "Polka" from *Age of Gold.*

And finally, so that children may see and touch, as well as listen, the teacher invites a parent or an older student to sing or to play for the children, or takes the children on an excursion to hear instruments which cannot be transported. When the high school student brought her cello one morning and played for a few minutes, the children sat close so that they could see. They were charmed when she played a song they knew and immediately began to sing with her. Afterwards children crowded around to take turns at plucking the strings and listening to the buzzing tones—high and low.

Young children require only a few simple things in order to grow musically as best they can. They need *permission* and *opportunity to express themselves* in many musical ways, as a natural part of their everyday living. They need *time to explore* and to discover for themselves the singing, sounding, and rhythmically moving musical world that is theirs. And they need a teacher who is *an understanding musical companion* with both a high sense of adventure and a deep insight into children's musical development, to guide them happily upon the way.

## I. NEEDS RELATED TO GENERAL GROWTH CHARACTERISTICS

| CHILDREN NEED OPPORTUNITIES | THERE SHOULD BE | SUGGESTED MUSIC AND REFERENCES |
|---|---|---|
| 1. For physical activity<br>  *a.* Moving vigorously; with large muscles. | Self-initiated rhythmic movement. Songs, piano selections, and records inviting galloping, running, skipping, etc. | See page 35.<br>See *Subject Index, Free Rhythms, Large Muscle,* page 132. |
|   *b.* Moving calmly, precisely, with small muscles. | Finger plays, hand dramatizations. | See *Subject Index, Free Rhythms, Small Muscle,* page 132. |
|   *c.* Involving contrasts that develop coordination (slow and fast, light and heavy, etc.). | Story sequence of piano rhythms or songs or records. Expression of contrasts through use of suitable rhythmic instruments. | See pages 36, 43, 49, 54, 56-7, 62, 63, 65, 71.<br>See also *Rhythm Dramas,* suggested pages 54-5. |

| 2. For rest, following strenuous activity. | Calm quiet songs and records. Slow songs and records. Songs for teacher to sing to children. | See *Subject Index, Lullabies.* See *Records,* listed page 80. See NMH record "Sleepy Songs." |
|---|---|---|
| 3. For reliving experiences in the form of dramatic play. | Story-songs. Opportunities for improvising. Rhythmic and song dramatizations. Vocal imitations of animals and things. | See *Subject Index, Acting Out Life Experiences,* page 132. See *Tales with Tunes,* pages 84-94. See NMH record "Community Helpers." |
| 4. For growing into cooperative relationships. | Songs and rhythms about "me." Songs, story-songs, rhythmic dramatizations involving small groups and "taking turns." Antiphonal singing, teacher and class. Use of appropriate rhythm instruments to accompany songs and records. | See *Subject Index, Recognizing the Individual,* also *Family Living* and *Social Living.* Also pages 16, 41, 45, 59, 60-1, 62, 63. |
| 5. For satisfying curiosity. | Songs and rhythmic dramatizations about people and things. Individual experimentation with voice, simple instruments, rhythmic movement. | See *Subject Index, Guessing Games.* See suggestions, *Rhythm Dramas,* pages 54-5, *Instruments,* 67, *Moving with Music,* 35. |
| 6. For experiencing a wide range of need. | From nonsense songs to sleepy songs. From the joy of "Jingle Bells" to the calm tenderness of "Silent Night" and the lonesomeness of "Down in the Valley." From rhythmic dramatizations of the heavy tread of elephants to the pattering of dancing raindrops. | Animal Pictures, 49-53 Down in the Valley, 112 Jingle Bells, 69 Lonesome Dove, The, 46 Raindrops, 75 Silent Night, 114 Shanghai Chicken, 5 |
| 7. For expressing their own feelings in many spontaneous musical ways. | Freedom to make up chants and songs and rhythms and dances. | See stress on spontaneous music making, pages 21, 35, 67. |
| 8. For feeling at home with things that grownups regard as familiar. | Songs the whole family sings. Songs and rhythmic dramatizations about the immediate environment. | See Chapter VIII, 109-116, also pages 100-1, 105, 106, 107. See NMH records "Transportation" and "Community Helpers." |

## II. NEEDS RELATED TO CHILDREN'S MUSICAL GROWTH

| CHILDREN NEED OPPORTUNITIES | THERE SHOULD BE | SUGGESTED MUSIC AND REFERENCES |
|---|---|---|
| 1. For moving rhythmically in their own way, before adjusting to set musical patterns. | Individual experimentation with movement and instruments. Teacher adds percussion or piano accompaniment to fit child's tempo. | See pages 35, 55, 67. For help in providing accompaniments, see pages 117, 118, 119-124. |
| 2. For moving at faster tempos before conforming to slower tempos. | Piano selections, records, songs, inviting faster rhythmic movement than adults normally require. | See *Drumming,* page 118, also *Accompanying Rhythmic Movement,* page 122. |
| 3. For singing for pure enjoyment. | Songs of many moods. Familiar songs chosen by children. Making-up songs. | See notes on child voice, page 125. |
| 4. For use of intervals they find easiest in singing and chanting. | Songs containing descending thirds, upward moving perfect fourths, upward moving major thirds. Songs and melodies built on pentatonic scales. | (This consideration has governed selection of songs for this book.) |
| 5. For use of spontaneous chanting to accompany large physical movements. | Freedom to chant as children move about. Encouragement by teacher of chant, through use of children's own chants. | See pages 21, 26. |
| 6. For visual-motor-vocal-auditory associations of up and down. | Vocal sound effects and chants in dramatic play, such as teeter-totter, swinging, etc. Spontaneous singing at play. Songs dealing with bouncing ball, climbing, etc. | Bouncing Balls, 38 Jungle Gym, 40 *Listening suggestions,* 82 Song for Swinging, 40 |

# When Company Comes

BY MARY JARMAN NELSON

The following program is a good framework for any Open House. Parents justifiably like to see their children performing happily and unselfconsciously. The unit here suggested provides a variety of sound and movement. The children planned the program, including refreshments. The teacher had printed the outline on a big piece of newsprint.

## OPEN HOUSE

### WHAT THEY DID

1. *Songs We Like*
   The children chose four songs to sing which they specially liked. While singing, they sat on the floor in a semicircle, just as they do during their daily "song time." One song, which brought in every child's name, was created by the group.

2. *Our Favorite Dance*
   The children wanted to show their parents how to willowbee. (See page 65.) This was a good choice because it gave individuals a chance to move creatively.

3. *We Play For You*
   The children had created an orchestration of *Boutique Fantasque*, page 70. After they had finished each child gave his instrument to one of his parents, and the PARENTS played.

   At this point one of the children requested that he be allowed to play a piece on the piano. He played *Rudy, Rudy, Rannie* on the black keys. The teacher suggested that four other children join him at the piano. While the five played, all the children sang the song.

4. *A Game For Everybody*
   The children then acted out *Who's That Knocking at My Door*, page 14. Before long some of the parents were asked to join the circle. Of course the child whose turn it was knocked at his father's "door."

5. *A Favorite Story*
   The children chose to dramatize *Chicken Licken*, page 88. There was a king who sat on a throne and watched. The costumes were very simple, hats and paper feathers for wings and tails. All the children sang the song while some acted the parts.

6. *Surprise!*
   A mother who played the violin had agreed to come and play to surprise the children. Her husband accompanied her on the guitar. After they played a gypsy dance, one little boy said, "Why don't you play a song we know?"

7. *Everybody Sing*
   *Oh! Susanna*, page 110, and *The Marines' Hymn*, page 116, were chosen because parents were bound to know these songs.

### MUSIC THAT COULD BE USED

*Everybody's Welcome*, page 112.
*Today Is Parent's Day*, page 96 (with words adapted for the occasion).
*Oh, Daddy Be Gay*,* page 13.
*Counting Song*,* page 8.

Especially effective for guests are:
*Bow, Belinda*, page 64.
*Old Brass Wagon*,* page 64.
*Bouncing Balls* (activity suggested page 38).
*Guess What Animal?* (Use *Animal Sketches*, page 49.)

So that the parents know what to do, when their turn comes, it is desirable to use a song that the children can sing as the parents play. See *Burlesque Band*, page 68, and *The Orchestra*, page 72.

(Individuals often wish to sing or play alone for people. If the group agrees, and if the child does not monopolize the time, this is a good experience.)

Other games in which parents can join are:
*Two in the Middle*,* page 30.
*One Day One Foot Kept Moving*,* page 42.
*My Mother Sent Me*,* page 45.
*The Old Brass Wagon*,* page 64.

Any favorite story may be play-acted, with music. Possibilities include *The Tired Giant*, page 71, and *The Gingerbread Man*, page 93.
A rhythm drama like "On the River" (described on page 55) is also very effective.

*Dolly's Lullaby*, page 12, might well be suggested in response to a child's request, because it is easy to sight-read. If both instruments play the melody, the second instrument beginning as the first instrument plays the second measure (canon-style), the children will have a nice surprise indeed.

It's polite to ask guests what *their* favorites are.

* Indicates availability of records made for use with this book.

Larger units which could occupy the major portion of an Open House program may be built by grouping familiar songs or activities around a central core of interest, preferably one related to the life experiences of the children themselves. Children who attend county fairs would enjoy organizing a fair in their classroom, replete with balloons, popcorn, and animals,—sung about and impersonated. Or perhaps a "Trip to the Circus" would fit in best with things the children have been thinking about, with animals in cages (see *Variations on a Walk*, page 56) and animal acts featured on the circus program, with a galaxy of tumbling clowns.

## A TRIP TO THE SEASHORE

*A dramatization with songs and movement*

| | ACTIVITY | MUSIC |
|---|---|---|
| 1. *Getting ready* | Silent pantomime; packing bags, fixing lunch, etc. May be accompanied by dialogue children have created. | |
| 2. *Some go on the train* | Form a train; passengers in coach hang from straps, swing to and fro. | *Let's Take a Little Trip,* page 23. (See also page 54.) |
| 3. *Some go in automobiles* | Sit on floor and pretend to drive, or use autos they have built of boxes. | *Our Windshield Wiper*, page 22. Or percussion or piano music as accompaniment. |
| 4. *Walking in the sand* | High stepping; lengthening out and slackening as shoes fill with sand. | *Walking in the Sand*, page 36. Percussion or piano. |
| 5. *Digging in the sand* | Imaginary shovels; big shovels used in standing position, small ones used in squatting position. Three or four children around each sandpile. | *Digging in the Sand*, page 36. Percussion or piano. |
| 6. *Throwing pebbles in the water* | Swinging arm and torso motions, with sharp release. | *Throwing Seashells*, page 37. |
| 7. *Jumping over piles of sand* | One pile of sand; children line up and take turns running for about ten feet, then leaping. | Percussion accompaniment which follows the movement. |
| 8. *Going into the water* | Running or tiptoeing to meet waves; then running back again. | Piano improvisation or percussion accompaniment. |
| 9. *Resting in the sun* | Children stretch out on floor; relax and close their eyes. | *Rest Song*, page 27. |

The charm of these presentations for "company" lies in the natural and spontaneous manner in which the children sing, speak, and move. Repeated drill spoils the fun for everybody. For continuity, the teacher or a child chosen by the group might insert informal remarks preceding each section of the foregoing unit,—"Now we're going to walk in the sand" or "This is the way we run in and out of the water." Sometimes the group may prefer to have the company *guess* what it is doing,—"This is what all children like to do at the beach. Can you guess what we're doing?"

The performance of any of these units should be kept flexible. Children will want to make suggestions and requests. Even the day that company comes, the program may take an unexpected turn. One group discovered something on the seashore at the last minute, some animals which escaped from the circus and came for a swim.

People of all ages like to have company. We like to have our friends drop in unexpectedly and share our everyday experiences—our toys, our food, our music. A parent may drop in with a visitor from out of town, with whom your children will be glad to share their joy in music. When the piano tuner comes, the children will want to show him to what good use they put the piano, in return for his kindness in showing them how the hammers can be seen playing the piano strings, when the front boards are off. We also like to have company at special times, for whom we plan and prepare. The area of music offers children in the pre-school a valuable social experience in entertaining.

# CLASSIFIED INDICES

# RHYTHMIC INDEX

132

# Index of Song Titles and First Lines

Italics have been used to indicate the page numbers of songs and the first lines of songs. Other numbers indicate reference material.

52

134